Female Privileges in America!
Exposing Feminist Hypocrisy!

1. Published by
   Kindle Direct Publishing
   410 Terry Avenue,
   Seattle, Washington 98109-5210
2. ISBN: 9798547427350

Neither the publishers nor the author are engaged in rendering professional advice or services to the individual reader. The ideas, procedures, and suggestions contained in this book are not intended as a substitute for consulting with a physician. All matters regarding your health require medical supervision. Neither the author nor the publishers shall be liable or responsible for any loss or damage allegedly arising from any information or suggestion in this book. All Rights Reserved. 2022.

Female Privileges in America!
Exposing Feminist Hypocrisy!

-Introduction-

First and foremost, reading discretion is advised. If you're a feminist (you claim to be independent but you won't get your hands dirty and do dangerous jobs as men or do physical labor/work as hard as men but yet complain of unfair wages), or an average typical (obese, entitled woman who has short hair, who is cheap on dates, and also, unfaithful, lazy, and who alway's continue to play the victim when your caught cheating) American woman, you will feel insulted and you will resent almost everything (if not everything) in this book. This book is written for three purposes!

- *Expose the majority of American women on how selfish, egotistical, controlling, manipulative, useless, opportunistic, uncaring, and delusional they act, are, and proud to be.*
- *Encourage men to stay away from long-term relationships (living with them) with American women; and especially to never trust or marry them even if children are involved.*
- *Prove beyond a reasonable doubt that women would never survive or enjoy their current life luxuries (even today) and abundance without all the discoveries and inventions that men have created and discovered that women take advantage of today for their own uses which would contradict their "philosophy" of being*

Female Privileges in America!
Exposing Feminist Hypocrisy!

"independent" because if women were independent from the beginning of time, they would have made all of the discoveries and inventions that they use today (the automobile, the cell phone, the internet, the computer, the television, the air conditioner, the stove, the microwave, the refrigerator, and the list goes on) rather than men who discovered and/or invented all these beautiful luxuries that we use and operate today. What does this mean? Women can never be equal to men no matter how hard they try, or how much they think that they can! The results speak for themselves. Men are logical, women are emotional. Men are less likely to give up on something or someone, while women are more likely to quit and give up on something and someone. A perfect example of this would be the institution of marriage. Women are so fixated on getting married by giving clues, suggestions, and ideas to their boyfriends prior to getting married. The majority of American women at some point in their lives (usually when their getting older) crave and desire marriage. They give the first impressions and usually the first conversation involving the topic (toxic) of marriage. Once the man marries her, more than 90% of the time, the woman is so quick to run away and file for divorce! So much for "until death do us part!" By the way, for any woman reading this sentence and wants to say that the main reason why women file for divorce against their husband is that "they won't put up with men's crap anymore," please explain to yourself and to the world

Female Privileges in America!
Exposing Feminist Hypocrisy!

why lesbians divorce at a much higher rate than gay married men! What's the explanation for that? The answer is because women are so emotional and quick to give up and run away from their problems without fixing them or attempting to learn something from them and are so fixated on revenge and being vindictive (in a cowardly way) that to them marriage is a financial benefit whether the marriage works out (someone paying her bills and expenses) or not (alimony) for them. Not all, but the majority of American women are like this now!

Prove me wrong!

I wish that I was wrong! It's one of those opinions and beliefs that any rational thinking man would wish that every woman of theirs was traditional (cooked and cleaned for them, and was faithful towards their providing boyfriend/husband), but this is not the case and the facts are that the majority of American women who desire and complain about "not being equal to men and being paid less than men and don't benefit more than men" are absurd and false accusations. Women will always benefit financially (through marriage and divorce) more than any man can receive from these same circumstances. The whole point of this book is to prove and proclaim why modern American women expect men to be traditional and yet refuse to be traditional themselves! Enjoy the facts, everyone! This book is intended to be a life-lesson for men

Female Privileges in America!
Exposing Feminist Hypocrisy!

to read, embrace, accept, and understand that as they grow older, unless technology is strictly limited (no internet or television) that women will "generally" behave barbaric and opportunistic against you (using you for your money to only benefit themselves because these women believe that they're more valuable than anything else that exists on this planet. This book is also dedicated to women to teach them that one day men, will no longer put up with your abusive bullshit and that one day, when baby-boomers leave either most or all political offices in this country, and millenial men step in (or younger generations in the future), one by one, your rights will be taken away; and although you will protest against these measures, all the millenial men that you hurt will never forget all the damage that you have done to them. Women are no doubt vindictive; but men with balls can be vindictive as well and that is what this book is all about! Make no mistake about that! The time is coming for men to once again take over and lead this planet again without women interfearance which has demonstrated nothing but poor leadership. This book is dedicated to all of the men who have suffered from women's lies, deception, opportunistic actions, and who were raised by mothers who never warned them about women's bullshit about potentially using them (their own sons) for money, child support, alimony, and other benefits that women can legally steal from men thanks to biased & sexist judges!

Female Privileges in America!
Exposing Feminist Hypocrisy!

I
-Women make less than men-

This first chapter will solely focus on the many reasons why women are nowhere near as qualified to earn the same equal amount of pay for equal work as men receive. Many women may disagree after reading this chapter, but facts will be presented and facts don't lie. Let's begin with a typical chart displaying that men get paid more than women.

The Gender Pay Gap

	Men	Women	
$1.00		enter low-paying careers	$0.10
$0.90		care for kids	$0.04
$0.80		are women	$0.09
$0.70			
$0.60			
$0.50			

Allegedly, life is unfair to women because there's a huge conspiracy for almost every employer/business/corporation to

Female Privileges in America!
Exposing Feminist Hypocrisy!

specifically single out women from receiving equal pay as men receive for the same work/labor that is performed from both of these genders. Apparently, these businesses owners/human resources agents/managers conspire together to be sexist and hire a man and a woman for the same position in order to pay a woman a shorter wage while a man gets to keep 20-30 more cents for every dollar that a woman earns. The results of this is that for women, for every dollar that they make, they will receive 20-30 cents less than men. According to delusional/feminist American women, this is unfair, sexist, biased, cruel, appalling, and contradicts the clear definition of equality in the United States Constitution (as if the majority of women in the United States who are American feminists actually read the entire Constitution and understand its principles). But there is a problem with the women who believe in this false logic and/or anybody who believes in this nonsense. Here is a chart to make my first primary example (of many) of showing why men make more money than women.

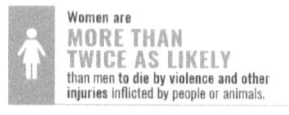

In the U.S., men are **12 TIMES MORE LIKELY** than women to be fatally injured in the workplace.

Women are **MORE THAN TWICE AS LIKELY** than men to die by violence and other injuries inflicted by people or animals.

AVERAGE NUMBER OF FATAL INJURIES PER 1 MILLION WORKING PEOPLE

RANK	MEN	WOMEN
1	Wyoming (210.9)	Nebraska (17.1)
2	Alaska (165.8)	Arkansas (11.3)
3	Montana (140.1)	Wisconsin (11.2)
4	South Dakota (128.6)	West Virginia (11.1)
5	North Dakota (122.5)	Mississippi (9.9)

Female Privileges in America!
Exposing Feminist Hypocrisy!

This source is from the Bureau of Labor Statistics. This graph was generated and studied by multiple experts and analysts who have studied and continue to study the never-ending worker's compensation cases, promote the welfare and protection for people who are seeking employment, protecting equal pay, protecting healthcare, and other employee benefits. However, this chart was done by economists who are personally trained and granted access to communicate with civilians (employees/former employees) either in person, by phone, by mail, or online. This is how they gather their data to create and generate the above chart through a typical engagement of occupational-requirements-survey-respondents. In other words, this chart was calculated based on volunteers of current employees and former employers who aided the Bureau of Labor Statistics to form this study. Now, on the top-left corner of the chart, in green font writing, the chart clearly states that "12 million men are more likely than women to be fatally injured in the workplace." What is the reason for this? Is it because men are less careful? Is it because men ignore safety rules more than women? All of these actions could relate to some men. The author has worked in several warehouses, restaurants, offices, janitorial services, and more. In other words, the author has observed men and his own actions related to these accusations. Women do it all the time too. But that's not the point. The point is and the real reason why men get paid more is because they do way more dangerous jobs than women; and even the women in government know this, which is why they never author, promote, or attempt to pass legislations for equal pay because

Female Privileges in America!
Exposing Feminist Hypocrisy!

these women politicians don't either care, or realize that they get paid more (with better benefits) than the average middle-class male which these politicians are supposed to be compassionate, protect, and render welfare towards any gender (money, benefits, reparations). For a woman politician to advocate equal pay for women, would only label themselves (the politicians) a hypcrocrite because again, these women politicians get paid more than middle-class women. The arguement to this fact may be by delusional women that ignore obvious facts:

"a politician is not a waiter and a server is not a politician. Of course, there's going to be wage differences. But don't these positions (a restaurant worker and a politician) help to serve and communicate with the public? The answer is yes. So what does this have to do with women earning less? What does politics have to do with this? Everything! Women politicians and several opportunistic male politicians, who never attempt to legislate any bills to establish equal pay for women, yet promote the idea usually during their campaign speeches will go as far as that but never beyond. But again, it's not the male politicians fault. Talk is cheap, actions speak! Men get injured 12 more times than women on the job because, men are more likely to seek employment with construction (constructing houses/buildings/automobiles), being a fisherman (catching seafood for the supermarkets), and hunting (hunting animals so those animals can eventually be distributed by other means to supermarkets, retail outlets, and even the zoo if the purpose is to capture the animal). Now, on the top-right portion of the graph in red font-writing, it states that: "women are more

Female Privileges in America!
Exposing Feminist Hypocrisy!

twice as likely than men to die by violence and other injuries inflicted by people or animals." In other words, the only indication and study that a woman's life is in danger from animals is if she somehow has an occupation where it involves being in the woodlands/forest/jungle/woods, etc. Unfortunately, even though they are twice as likely to be injured and/or killed by humans and/or animals than men, that still does not discredit the lesser-half portion of men who are in the same job field and also get injured and/or killed by humans and animals. In other words, women-only can defeat men in the work field by being assaulted/killed by humans and animals rather than doing more harder work than men. Men climb ladders and fall off. Electricians (the majority of them in this field are men) sometimes get electrocuted by repairing utility pools. How many mechanics have gotten injured changing a woman's engine because she may have failed to put the necessary engine oil inside that is required for the car to function? Note: The majority of American women never lift up their car-hood and place the appropriate fluids that their vehicle needs in order to remain operable and reliable. This suggests that American women are not keen on getting their hands dirty, at least the majority of them. There is always an exception to the rule but facts speak for themselves. This also suggests that since American women are only fixated on driving cars and not maintaining them; or repairing them on their own, that men have to step in and apply for the position of a lube technician or a mechanic. Most of these applications are filled out by men, and most of these jobs are given to and doen by men. It's a dirty, dangerous, and rewarding career. I

Female Privileges in America!
Exposing Feminist Hypocrisy!

always wondered why women don't want these jobs! The truth of the matter is, women don't want to do excessive work. American women want the same pay as a man but a lot less responsibilities for the same job. Do you ever wonder why is it when you go to an airport, and the moment that you enter your airplane, all of the pilots are almost always a man? The reason why is because piloting can be accepted as a dangerous occupation. How about roofing? How many women apply for that job? What about sewer workers (city workers who go inside the sewers to connect and/or repair sewage lines connections to people's homes)? How many American women will apply for that job? How many women work and apply for transporting heavy merchandise/produce by driving trucks? The answers to all of these questions are a very small margin. Too low when compared to male applicants and workers. Of course, all of these jobs pay exceedingly well. For example, you may go to a car dealership and come across a woman who attempts to sell you the very same car that she is persistent on selling and probably would drive herself, but would never assemble that same car (that was assembled in a factory) herself no matter how good the pay generally is. To that woman, talking and selling is hard enough work. Let the mouth do the talking and not the hands! This is the mentality of a typical waitress at a restaurant. Only bring food to the client, and expect tips! Forget about washing dishes or being a cook! Women in restaurants would rather quit than engage in these physical labor requirements. For the record, the author has worked at 29 restaurants and has yet to see a white-liberal dishwasher who was a woman in Los Angeles, California. If

Female Privileges in America!
Exposing Feminist Hypocrisy!

you don't believe me, you are more than welcome to do your own investigation on this. Almost all dishwashers are men and hispanic; and lucky to be an American. The typical waitress is usually lazy, selfish, and entitled; and will never extend a hand to help unless there is a reason to do so. They will do less physical labor than men in a restaurant, and demand more money or pay, and usually receive more compensation and free food (than the typical back of the house employee receives) which is more benefits than what a male dishwasher will ever receive. Talk about equality right? But this is just an example. There are many more. The point of the matter is that women get paid less for every dollar that a man makes because they are unwilling to apply for occupations that men currently possess and may not desire but are willing to do the work in order to get paid more because the man does not have a choice. Back-breaking physical labor does not attract women because they know that they will have to either get their hands dirty (which they don't want) or have a reliable open schedule (which they don't have because many of these women have kids) for these kinds of jobs. Therefore, facts speak for themselves. For every woman and feminist reading this, let me remind you:

- *Women want convenient work environments (little to no physical labor and air-conditioned environments)*
- *Women want special privileges in the work environment more than men.*
- *Women will almost never volunteer to stay overtime in order to receive compensation. They typically have the*

Female Privileges in America!
Exposing Feminist Hypocrisy!

same excuse, "I have children, I'm a single mom, I can't or I'm too busy!" To the eyes and ears of upper management, these women are unreliable and cannot be depended upon. Men make fewer or no excuses to stay overtime!

- *Women want the benefits but not the responsibilities to those demanded benefits (equal pay, equal rights, special privileges, and authority)!*

Now let's examine, at least according to the United States Census Bureau, on how many women are very selective with their careers from 2019 (and even before and after that period).

Female Privileges in America!
Exposing Feminist Hypocrisy!

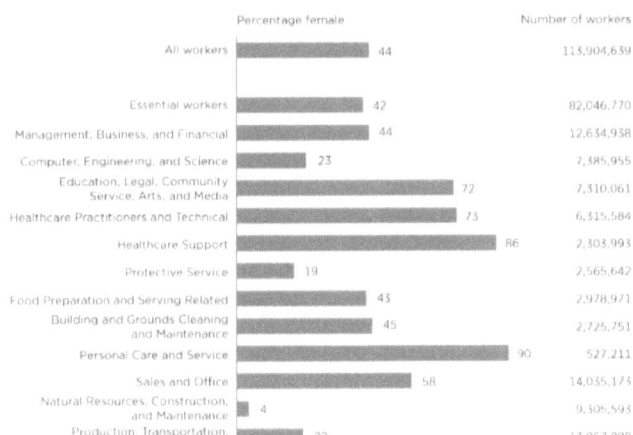

Just to make a point, and prove my point that men make more money than women is because they do more dangerous jobs; despite the fact that women populate the United States at a much more superior factor than men; look no further on this chart than "natural resources, construction, and maintenance" which is 4% of the women workforce unless the United States government is lying and deliberately manipulated this graph. In other words, the opportunity exists for women to drive on roads and bridges to get to their work or pick up their kids from school, and/or be employed in a building that was constructed and/or repaired by hard working men. According to this graph, "personal care and service"

Female Privileges in America!
Exposing Feminist Hypocrisy!

amounted to 90% of women. Personal care and service are not back-breaking and dangerous jobs that put your life at risk unless of course an individual attempts to rob or kill you which is obviously a crime which rarely happens in those professions; no matter what U.S. city or jurisdiction that you live in.

A lot of women claim to be hard-working women because they have children and therefore have to tend to them and work at the same time. At the same time, to be fair, nobody told these women to have children and bring upon an offspring that they struggle to maintain to pay for. That's their fault! There should be no sympathies for single mothers since at the end of the day, a pregnant woman has the final answer and decision to determine whether her child will be born and/or aborted. Men do not make those decisions. So, if these women earn less than men because they have children and depend, demand, and require the government to tend to their needs and disadvantages, that's not America's problem! Let me repeat that! That is not this country's problem! It goes back to the point that employers should and be required to work around a single mothers schedule in order to accommodate her and her child's needs; and if the employer doesn't, then they're discriminating against the irresponsible dependant woman. Here is a perfect example of "personal care and service jobs" which pay less than dangerous jobs and also proof that women choose to select lower wages intentionally (or subconsiousually) and complain about getting lower pay than men. Again, according to the U.S Bureau of statistics, giving full credence

Female Privileges in America!
Exposing Feminist Hypocrisy!

to their analysis and confirmation (as liberal feminists and democrats trust their own governments and studies and almost always believe that their government would never lie to them so long as their Democratic politicians)

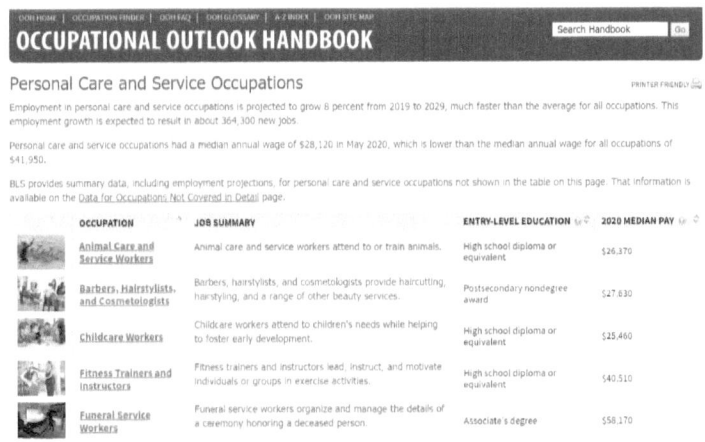

On average a woman selecting (intentionally) the 90% occupation of the women's work force of the "personal care and service positions" have the least amount of back-breaking labor of occupations. Let's take a look at some of these examples after stating the fact that women only make between $21,120-$41,950 annualy.

- *It does not take hard work to feed animals, take care of their waste; and be a service worker (animal care and service workers)'*

Female Privileges in America!
Exposing Feminist Hypocrisy!

Note: This is not intendend to insult people in these professions and/or occupations but to make several points that should be recognized and understood when comparing the facts and REASONS WHY WOMEN CHOOSE TO BE UNDERPAID IN THE UNITED STATES OF AMERICA!

- *It does not take back-breaking labor to cut an individuals hair, dye hair, or paint nails (barbers, hairstylists, and cosmetologists). Usually these women who work in these environments have air-conditioned atmospheres and usually stand in one or two positions to get the job done unlike men who work in construction and building houses and other buildings; and roads in general with no air conditioning.*
- *Again it does not take hard work to feed and possibly clothe children as a childcare worker. Single and married men do this all the time. What's the difference if women are doing this for a child that is not their biological offspring? How long does it take to cook eggs and serve milk? How long does it take to make spaghetti or fettucini? To be sure, I bet the average American woman feminist reading this does not even know how to make spaghetti and fettucini. Yet, they think that they're "wifey material."*
- *Childcare workers! I hope that's true because never before in history have women lost their children in the United States to their respected states because they (the women) refuse to provide for their own children*

Female Privileges in America!
Exposing Feminist Hypocrisy!

economically, cook, and clean for them because they feel that it's an inferior position for them even though in the animal kingdom it's been done since the beginning of time and for the human race in historical times and should be practiced in our modern times. If the author is wrong about this, please search the internet when there are questions on why "women won't cook and clean in the United States for their men?" Women do typically respond "that men should have to cook and clean for themselves and that this is not the 1950's anymore and economic times have changed which (are excuses really from these lazy-feminist women)!" Yet, in these expensive economic times as these lazy women claim to live in, should men still have to pay for dates and transportation just to take them out and pay for the privilege for these women's time? Fuck no!

The author agrees with this ideology but disagrees with American women's notion and mentality that a man should have to pay for dates (when taking her out), pick them up (spending money on gas), and having to give away more than half of property and investments after a divorce (businesses of all kinds) that the woman did nothing to earn or invest in; yet demands and expects equal payment and benefits just for the sake of being married to the man who received his right-earned benefits. In other words, the woman did not work hard or contributed of any kind (there is an exception to the rule which is a very few selected) to the prosperous business; yet feels entitled to benefit from it, as if the marriage should

Female Privileges in America!
Exposing Feminist Hypocrisy!

not work out. So much for these American women being independent as they claim right?

- *Fitness trainers and instructors! The author almost wants to laugh at this because American women are generally obsese to begin with at least according to the Center For Disease and Control And Prevention:*

Data from the National Health and Nutrition Examination Survey

- In 2017-2018, the age-adjusted prevalence of obesity in adults was 42.4%, and there were no significant differences between men and women among all adults or by age group.
- The age-adjusted prevalence of severe obesity in adults was 9.2% and was higher in women than in men.
- Among adults, the prevalence of both obesity and severe obesity was highest in non-Hispanic black adults compared with other race and Hispanic-origin groups.
- The prevalence of severe obesity was highest among adults aged 40-59 compared with other age groups.
- From 1999-2000 through 2017-2018, the prevalence of both obesity and severe obesity increased among adults.

Obesity is associated with serious health risks (1). Severe obesity further increases the risk of obesity-related complications, such as coronary heart disease and end-stage renal disease (2,3). From 1999-2000 through 2015-2016, a significantly increasing trend in obesity was observed (4). This report provides the most recent national data for 2017-2018 on obesity and severe obesity prevalence among adults by sex, age, and race and Hispanic origin. Trends from 1999-2000 through 2017-2018 for adults aged 20 and over are also presented.

prevalence of obesity among adults by race and Hispanic origin in 2017-2018?

What was the prevalence of severe obesity among adults in 2017-2018?

What are the trends in obesity and severe obesity among adults?

Summary

Definition

Data source and methods

About the authors

References

Suggested citation

This study from the CDC (if they're accurate because they were wrong many times about Covid-19 & the Covid-19 vaccine) states that men and women are generally obese based on a percentage of an average of 42.4%. In other words, men and women in the United States are over 1/3rd obese in America. What does this mean and what is the point? Here is

Female Privileges in America!
Exposing Feminist Hypocrisy!

the point! The point is that gyms across the United States will not employ obese women (or men) to make an example of positive health and fitness; since generally, American women gain weight and do nothing about their weight or health unless of course these women are actressess (which may compromise their ability to obtain a contract to be a part of the film and/or music industry) or because they are in the wrestling atmosphere (UFC which is an exception to the rule) or trying to marry some poor sap to pay her bills, but generally American woman are obese because they give up on themselves and refuse to maintain their health and fitness (generally before finding some idiot to marry them). So the question remains "how can an average American fitness instructor and/or trainer make a lot of money when they work so hard to lift weights and do physical labor?" The reason why is because these women who do this are an exception to the rule. No matter how many commercials that Americans see of women being in perfect shape in grocery stores or in other environments, it's nowhere near the truth in reality. Prove me wrong feminists! Go ahead and see how many obese women are shopping for groceries at the supermarket (in your jurisdiction) at 10:00 a.m. and write a book about proving me wrong.

- *Funeral service workers are another typical occupation for women. But are they working hard to deserve this position and be compensated for such hard work?*

Female Privileges in America!
Exposing Feminist Hypocrisy!

If women who work in cemeteries have the position of being a "funeral service worker" it's because they are selling funeral arrangements and tombstones to clients! That's right! They do nothing to operate a tractor and dig the grave (which is physical labor) to place the deceased corpse in its proper and reserved burial space. Don't believe me? Go to your nearest cemetery and see how many women dig and cover graves for their clients! Almost all of these individuals who operate tractors and use construction equipment to bury deceased corpses are men! That's why these men get paid more, even though they work harder than these women who make money with their mouths selling graves and burial space (like most sales people of all kinds and politicians) rather than their hands (through physical labor and not signing paperwork). Again, prove the author wrong and see how many women are willing to grab a shovel and dig a hole to make a grave or use a tractor or any construction equipment to conclude their job (in establishing proper burials) in over 100 degree weather. Almost all American (especially feminist) women will not do this because they think that they deserve better work conditions than to work in these work environments and atmospheres. The hypocrisy speaks for itself! Women in other countries (Vietnam, China, & Mexico) get paid less than America women but will almost never have problems or complain about sewing, cooking, cleaning, or doing physical labor to make ends meet. The point being is that American women are spoiled, entitled; and desire ultimate benefits but desire to render less than basic or the bare minimum responsibilities to earn those benefits. Prove the author wrong for the perceived reputation of

Female Privileges in America!
Exposing Feminist Hypocrisy!

American women. American women complain about not receiving "equal pay" when comparing themselves to men, which is only by gender, and not by any work ethics. There is an exception to the rule in this; but in general and most circumstances, women will work less and engage in less dependability than men; and yet will bitch and complain about not receiving equal pay when compared to men. However, let's assume as Americans, that feminist women in America are correct. Let's give these idiots the benefit of the doubt. Let us be nice and say that men earn more than women because they hate to see women earn the same as them, because these men are jealous and vindictive (like women after divorcing a man who wants more than 50% of everything that he earned without her assistance). As it is, most feminist women who demand "equal pay and benefits" (yet refuse the same responsibilities that women were expected to receive in previous decades for their work ethic is cook, clean, and work in hot temperatures with their hands) are hypocritical liberals and socialists depending on the geographical jurisdiction that these women generally tend to reside in (California, Washington, Oregon, and New York are the worst states in the country). Generally, these feminists select to live and reside in Democratic cities, counties, and states, because they know that these jurisdictions will grant them their ears and accept their false premises and arguments. Why is it false, you might ask? Here is the reason why! Liberal feminists, who are more than likely to identify themselves as Democrats and/or socialist Democrats (the Bernie Sanders supporters) will complain, tarnish, and attack (verbally) billionaire's because they make

Female Privileges in America!
Exposing Feminist Hypocrisy!

too much money (yet these same Democrats refuse to open their own businesses or attempt to make/create any entrepreneurship on their behalf and yet complain on why business owners make more money than them). In other words, nothing stops these hypocritical Democratic/Socialist women from benefiting from the laws of Capitalism in the United States of America. Yet again, let's prove the feminists right! If they hate billionaire's so much for probably inventing and discovering the very same inventions and/or technology that these same women use, operate, and take advantage today, then let's reevaluate their argument on why billionaire's allegedly rip people off in the United States and intentionally deprive American women (whether their feminist or not) of fair compensation wages. If these same billionaire's benefit today by engaging in their current practices, and get away with paying low taxes, and compensating women inferior wages compared to men, because of "alleged loophole laws" then let's use this same argument which is used by Democrats and feminists. Let's believe these feminists that these billionaires pay a lower tax because of loopholes and other advantages that are legally or illegally given to them. But if these billionaires really are fixated on depriving women of "equal pay" why is that???

"If corporations could get away with compensating women less money than men, why do they not hire only women (or the majority of women for their corporations) instead of men (to save money) since women could earn less money than men

Female Privileges in America!
Exposing Feminist Hypocrisy!

which will/should/could benefit these corporations economically?" - The author of this book

There is no conspiracy in this matter! Feminists are stupid and ignorant to realize this fact and arguement. The feminist movement's only argument that women receive less money than men is a nonsense claim that "patriarchy sexism exists through domination from men against women." However, there's no proof of this conspiracy; and as much as I feel obligated to remind all of my readers this, consistently throughout this book in repetitive examples and methods, that the obvious method and opportunity that the majority of American women can do in order to improve their economic circumstances, is to open up small businesses (which generates at least half if not more of America's Gross Domestic Product and therefore helps stabilize the economy) and hire more women, and give them a decent and generous wage. Unfortunately, while women are opening more small businesses today than ever before in American history, many women still hesitate and just plain out refuse to explore the opportunity of being a self-made business owner. According to the women's business owner statistics, this chart was generated from them acknowledging (as of 2021) the existence of women entrepreneurs; and the nine million people their businesses generally employ and how much revenue these women-owned businesses generated in sales and/or services, a whopping 1.7 trillion dollars in sales.

Female Privileges in America!
Exposing Feminist Hypocrisy!

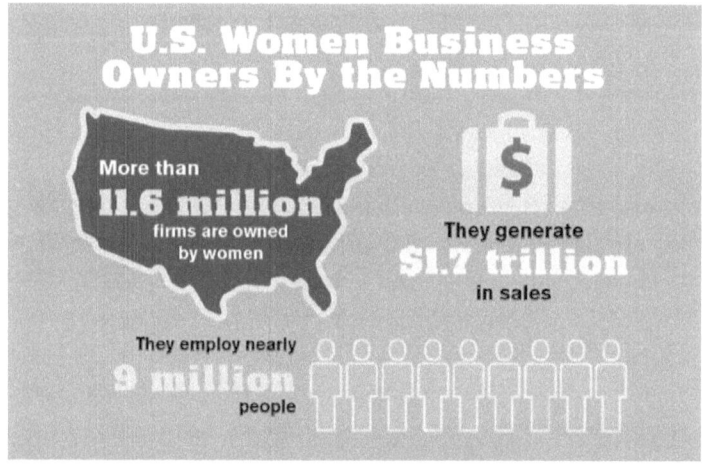

Now, according to the latest 2020 United States Census population, the female population (I'm not including transgenders because their irrelevant and I also believe that transgenders cannot biologically alter their sex, as I believe in only two genders which is male and female) outnumbers the male population. There are more women in the United States than there are men. This is a fact! Now, since women dominate men in terms of only the population on planet Earth, when it comes to demographics, why don't the majority of adult women in the United States dominate men in the entrepreneur-status and open up more businesses so they can finally get the credit for primarily stabilizing the economy (in regards to generating revenue for the country) more than men? Why don't women take more initiative, effort, drive, passion, and ambition to change the economy in their favor? Nothing stops them from

Female Privileges in America!
Exposing Feminist Hypocrisy!

doing so except themselves. The courts and politicians are already on their side; so what obstacles do they face? Here is a published article that appeared on CNBC by Rohit Arora; the CEO of biz2credit.com.

 Why male entrepreneurs in the US make double their female counterparts

The average annual revenues of women-owned business rose 68% in 2019, to $384,359 from $228,578 in 2018, according to the annual study of women-owned companies by Biz2Credit.

However, while this growth is impressive, male-owned businesses generated a much higher average annual revenue: $752,154 in 2019, up jump from $473,157 in 2018. In direct comparison, firms owned by men made $367,795 more revenue on average than women-owned businesses last year, according to Biz2Credit research, which examined 30,000 companies nationwide in more than 20 industries, including retail, health care, hospitality, construction and professional services, among others.

The number of women-owned businesses that applied for funding in 2019 increased slightly, although their average loan amounts went down from $48,341 to $40,513 in 2019. The most common type of funding was working capital.

The study also found that while the average credit score for women-owned businesses increased from 588 in 2018 to 590 in 2019, they trailed the scores of their male counterparts (613) by 23 points.

According to this published web-page, women are stepping it up (finally) on becoming self-made business owners. However, this article implies and confirms that even women-owned businesses who generate an annual revenue of an average $384,359.00 is still less than what men received in annual revenues when compared to an estimated amount of $752,154.00. This confirms that small business owners who are owned by men make more money than small businesses that are owned by women. I'm not disputing that! But what this article fails to mention is the real reason why women are

Female Privileges in America!
Exposing Feminist Hypocrisy!

earning less. Here is the only argument that the article has; it's literally ridiculous!

 Why male entrepreneurs in the US make double their female counterparts

> The male advantage can be attributed to the fact that they have been in business longer, and these entrepreneurs have had time to develop strong networks in industries like IT, construction and logistics. But economists predict that in a few years female business owners should catch up to their male counterparts and things may start to even out.

First of all, small businesses of every kind and corporations of every kind can either thrive or fail. It's a dog-eat-dog world when it comes to businesses. That's how businesses stabilize themselves by either offering a better product/service, at a more affordable rate in addition to offering superior customer service than his or her competitor, or they can offer poor customer service, poor products and service, at a high price and watch themselves destroy everything that they created. Second of all, men are more likely to upgrade, expand their business, and even franchise their businesses nationally and internationally. Why? Because men are more determined and self-motivated than women and also do not have obstacles (pregnancies) that stop them from increasing and expanding their profits and opportunities when compared to women. Third of all, men are willing to save and invest for these potential circumstances and opportunities. Women rarely save and invest in anything. Women are generally characterized (thanks to stereotypes that they earned themselves) as being an "irresponsible spender" and thus spends more than what is absolutely necessary on herself and her image rather than things that are essential and necessary. Obviously, not all

Female Privileges in America!
Exposing Feminist Hypocrisy!

American women are this way, but the majority of them are, and just because a woman becomes an entrepreneur, it does not mean that she has removed her typical expectations of "feeling entitled" and "victimizing herself" for benefits and opportunities. These traits will remain with this average American woman regardless if she's wealthy or poor, and for the rest of her life. Fourth of all, a lot of women-owned business believes that she earns less because customers prefer to shop at businesses that are owned by men, in which I highly suggest for these delusional women to seek a psychiatrist to assist them in "fact checks" that male clients/customers are not out there to also deprive them economically like they think male employers are consistently trying to do to them in the work-field. There comes a point in your life where women should take responsibility for their decisions, actions, and failures. American women are not always victims! Let the feminist ideology accept this!

Note: Before I end this chapter, just to prove sexism clearly exists against men when compared to women in the federal government's work-field, here is a published web-page from the Selective Service System website under the section https://www.sss.gov/register/benefits-and-repercussions/*:*

Female Privileges in America!
Exposing Feminist Hypocrisy!

Federal Job Training

The Workforce Innovation and Opportunity Act (formerly the Workforce Investment Act (WIA)) offers programs that can train young men seeking vocational employment or enhancing their career. This program is only open to those men who register with Selective Service. Only men born after December 31, 1959, are required to show proof of registration.

Federal Jobs

A man must be registered to be eligible for jobs in the Executive Branch of the Federal Government and the U.S. Postal Service. Proof of registration is required only for men born after December 31, 1959.

This is an official declaration and warning for men who refuse to register for "Selective Service" that unless men are prepared and willing to give up their life during times of war, (which is to sacrifice their life to enrich banking-elites, defense contractors, oil-tycoons, and other pharmaceutical corporate elites, and other politicians stock-profits), then he (the man) is not eligible to work as the President's Press Secretary, or even be employed by the Secret Service to protect and defend the current president himself; or let's say the man only desires to be a chef for the President and cook his meals, he can't even make a sandwich for him unless he promises to sacrifice his life by registering for Selective Service. Yet a woman, does not have to put her life at risk and sacrifice her life for her country by registering for the Selective Service in order to potentially do the very same thing a man does and have the very same jobs; and protect the President as a Secret Service agent regardless if she is personally assigned to physically protect

Female Privileges in America!
Exposing Feminist Hypocrisy!

the President personally (which is unlikely). Because of her gender, women are allowed to obtain special treatment and as a result, they don't have to worry about putting their lives at risk when working directly or indirectly for the federal government in order to pay their bills. However, men do! This means that a mailman is twice as likely to die than a mail lady. How is that possible, you might ask? Because men that deliver mail to American citizens's homes every day (including Sunday's) have to already risk the everyday opportunity of some idiot crashing into his mail truck; and on top of that, his president can send his ass to war or into the military for any reason that potentially threatens national security against the United States. Mail lady's only have to worry about people crashing into their truck; and maybe a dog biting her and somebody mugging her for mail, but hey so do men. And yet, if both of these individuals (the mailman and the mail lady) have equal hourly wages, and work the same amount of hours, the woman gets the benefit of being excluded from leaving her job to go die in events of war. In Chapter 6, we will get more into details regarding "draft eligibility and exclusive female privilege in America regarding women in the military compared to men in the military." For now, let's move on to chapter 2 to prove more female privilege in America, if this chapter has not convinced you (the reader) yet of all the benefits and opportunities that women receive and get away with compared to men for the same jobs and/or benefits, proceed further to the next chapter!

Female Privileges in America!
Exposing Feminist Hypocrisy!

II

-Women benefit from marriage more than men-

When has a man ever benefited economically from marriage? There are exceptions to this rule! For example, Britney Spears (the alleged pop princess) had to pay alimony to Keven Federline because she made more money than him. Of course, she did because she was a famous pop singer in her time. However, and generally, men who "pop the question" to their woman who shields herself with a "mask of perfection and flawless characteristics" tend to reveal their authentic flawed beauty and characteristics to their man only after getting married. The average woman that an average man wanted to marry, is nothing in comparison to her actions, personality, and/or looks when the woman began dating her man that she eventually, yet prior before being married to her man somehow, suddenly, became completely different only after getting married to him. This implies that the woman was able to get her prey (the man) to propose and pop the question to "marry her" so that all of the benefits, rights, opportunities, and advantages ended for the man (in favor of the woman through divorce proceedings & alimony) who asked his girlfriend to marry him! The woman gains, benefits, and is entitled to everything! The woman generally wins economically (in court) while the man loses! The truth is that women know that these are the facts, and that is the reason why the majority of women in the United States desire and

Female Privileges in America!
Exposing Feminist Hypocrisy!

*crave marriage so much. These women (including feminists) know that courts are biased against men and will always be (so long as baby boomers are in charge of the courts) in favor of their requests, wants, and/or demands; and will generally always believe in their arguments (even though in many cases their arguments are impractical and illogical) because generally these judges who currently work in these courts had women in their generation (the silent generation and baby boomer generation) cook, clean, be submissive and give them everything that they want and desire, and therefore feel obligated in return to reciprocate back a favorable opportunity and response back to all women no matter what generation of women. In other words, these judges cannot see the flaws in women or their desire to steal money (legally) from men or even manipulate men in today's society as much. How can women do this after all? Women are pure and innocent at least the women in my generation, a typical baby boomer man would say to him or herself these expressions and with good reason since these women (in previous decades) are nothing like millenial and generation Z women who consistently are more capable of being unfaithful, lazy, entitled, vindictive, and does nothing to help the planet, at least generally for their benefit. Prove me wrong again! However, this chapter is special (like every other chapter) because it proves how many **advantages that women have** when compared to men; and yet these idiot feminists either deliberately fail to acknowledge this or by being vindicated against men, they choose to ignore this. What about men's rights? Let's take a closer look at my*

Female Privileges in America!
Exposing Feminist Hypocrisy!

argument about the prejudice and biased actions that the courts give women when compared to men.

"Men, do not marry or you will always lose and surrender more than half of everything that you worked hard for and created in your lifetime while your girlfriend did almost nothing to get your hard-earned money!"

Let's take a look at the benefits that women receive prior to getting married to their future husband.
Men pay for dates and other expenses (alcoholic beverages, food, and transportation). **Note: women almost never pay for food, drinks, gas and anything else on dates because they are cheap and expect men to be traditional (and pay for dates and everything else since they're the one inviting but when do women ever invite men for dates and pay for everything)? In other words, women refuse to be generous like men as they generally refuse to pay for food, drinks, gas, and everything else (that men pay for) and yet themselves (the typical American women) refuse to cook, clean and provide for a man which is total hypocrisy. In other words, these women want and demand benefits and expect men to be traditional only for their convenience but refuse equal responsibility (cooking and cleaning for their men).It's such hypocrisy which defines the Democratic party and feminists. Rules for thee, but not for me!**
Men have to spend money for transportation (gas & maintenance) for their vehicles if these men want to make a positive example of themselves to seek and marry an

Female Privileges in America!
Exposing Feminist Hypocrisy!

ungrateful woman (who probably isn't worth it) to be married to begin with. In other words, when will you see a woman ask a man out on a date, (I hope that you feminists are reading this) and pay for everything? It does not exist and many feminists will say that "it's the man's job to ask and pay for everything." If the author is wrong in saying these accusations, then why don't feminists ever confront women and declare "that more women should ask men out and pay for dates?" It does not happen because feminists want and desire advantages and opportunities without earning them as men do with hard work and determination." Prove the author wrong! Now, let's take a look at the divorce rate in the United States (in the year 2020 since the author cannot include 2021 since the current year has not ended) at least according to the Center For Disease Control that Democratic feminist-women seem to support (including vaccine mandates) and believe in the CDC because, why would the CDC be wrong or lie in these marriage statistics (or anything else) as they are about anything else such as Covid-19 vaccinations, according to these liberal Democratic feminists? Trust your government always if these unelected people (the Center for Disease Control) at least supported the Democratic Party and are in charge of the United States in all forms of office, that these feminst women believe in! However, let's prove the facts according to the CDC (the typical Democratic ally and dictator to feminists across America) and prove that feminists and Democrats cherry-pick everything in politics and reality to benefit their arguments and false agenda.

Female Privileges in America!
Exposing Feminist Hypocrisy!

Year	Divorces & annulments	Population	Rate per 1,000 total population
2019[1]	746,971	272,842,748	2.7
2018[1]	782,038	271,791,413	2.9
2017[1]	787,251	270,423,493	2.9
2016[2]	776,288	257,904,548	3.0
2015[3]	800,909	258,518,265	3.1
2014[3]	813,862	256,483,624	3.2
2013[3]	832,157	254,408,815	3.3
2012[4]	851,000	248,041,986	3.4
2011[4]	877,000	246,273,366	3.6
2010[4]	872,000	244,122,529	3.6
2009[4]	840,000	242,610,561	3.5
2008[4]	844,000	240,545,163	3.5
2007[4]	856,000	238,352,850	3.6
2006[4]	872,000	236,094,277	3.7
2005[4]	847,000	233,495,163	3.6
2004[5]	879,000	236,402,656	3.7
2003[6]	927,000	243,902,090	3.8
2002[7]	955,000	243,108,303	3.9
2001[8]	940,000	236,416,762	4.0
2000[8]	944,000	233,550,143	4.0

[1] Excludes data for California, Hawaii, Indiana, Minnesota, and New Mexico.
[2] Excludes data for California, Georgia, Hawaii, Indiana, Minnesota, and New Mexico.
[3] Excludes data for California, Georgia, Hawaii, Indiana, and Minnesota.
[4] Excludes data for California, Georgia, Hawaii, Indiana, Louisiana, and Minnesota.
[5] Excludes data for California, Georgia, Hawaii, Indiana, and Louisiana.
[6] Excludes data for California, Hawaii, Indiana, and Oklahoma.

According to the CDC, the author is forced to exclude several crucial states relevant to his argument. However, let's look at this chart and accept the findings of the CDC which states unequivocally that:
In the year 2019, in the United States of America, 746,971 American citizens decided to end their vows and seek divorce because the marriage was great in the beginning, but determined to fail in the future. So, who benefits from this, is

Female Privileges in America!
Exposing Feminist Hypocrisy!

the real question that remains? But the reader will find the answer very quickly by comparing this chart and reading the rest of this chapter. Let men confirm their ultimate suspicion on marriage and be reminded of their ultimate instincts that marriage was never meant to benefit them but only decided to benefit women under all circumstances. Let the feminists challenge and disagree with the facts after this!

Provisional number of marriages and marriage rate: United States, 2000-2019

Year	Marriages	Population	Rate per 1,000 total population
2019	2,015,603	328,239,523	6.1
2018	2,132,853	327,167,434	6.5
2017	2,236,496	325,719,178	6.9
2016	2,251,411	323,127,513	7.0
2015	2,221,579	321,418,820	6.9
2014[1]	2,140,272	308,759,713	6.9
2013[1]	2,081,301	306,136,672	6.8
2012	2,131,000	313,914,040	6.8
2011	2,118,000	311,591,917	6.8
2010	2,096,000	308,745,538	6.8
2009	2,080,000	306,771,529	6.8
2008	2,157,000	304,093,966	7.1
2007	2,197,000	301,231,207	7.3
2006[2]	2,193,000	294,077,247	7.5
2005	2,249,000	295,516,599	7.6
2004	2,279,000	292,805,298	7.8
2003	2,245,000	290,107,933	7.7
2002	2,290,000	287,625,193	8.0
2001	2,326,000	284,968,955	8.2
2000	2,315,000	281,421,906	8.2

[1]Excludes data for Georgia.
[2]Excludes data for Louisiana.

Note: Number and rate for 2016 has been revised due to revised figures for Illinois. Rates for 2001-2009 have been revised and are based on intercensal population estimates from the 2000 and 2010 censuses. Populations for 2010 rates are based on the 2010 census.

Out of 2,015,603 marriages in the United States of America in 2019, divorces (in the same year) were inevitably requested in the amount of 746,971 which mathematically would accumulate to 1,268,632 after proper divorces. To remind my readers, that after looking at these percentages, it would imply that divorces are common and seem to accumulate a high percentage of divorces when compared to marriages. As it is, if

Female Privileges in America!
Exposing Feminist Hypocrisy!

you multiply 746,971 (times 3), you get a mathematical equation of 2,240,913. The reason why this formula is brought up mathematically is because, if you count for the official account of marriages (according to the CDC if the Democrats and feminists want to believe them), then 2,015,603 Americans is less than 2,240,913 Americans. In other words, these statistics imply that at least 40%-50% of Americans seek divorce after getting married and yet this does not include American couples who are married and are miserable and tolerate marriage for financial benefits, environments, and/or economical circumstances. Thanking and crediting Pew Research for confirming this information, as well as the U.S. Census for these accurate statistics, that this chart below should confirm that beyond a reasonable doubt that women still receive alimony at a much higher rate than men, yet more men are paying alimony today than in 1979 when the United States Supreme Court desired and ruled to make alimony gender-neutral. According to this article, in 4 out of 10 households, women are the breadwinners (the primary income generator in her family) which would indicate and confirm that feminist women are wrong when they "imply based on their speeches and mentality" that men almost always make more money than women through sexism and biased gender actions. Apparently, 400,000 alimony cases in the United States result in only 3% of men getting alimony payments when compared to women. Why is this, the reader and typical feminist delusional might ask? The primary reason is because women are so fixated, determined, ambitious, and vindictive to take her ex-husband (or current husband) to court and request

Female Privileges in America!
Exposing Feminist Hypocrisy!

alimony payments at a high rate and for as long as she wants. Despite these women claiming independence and being independent, these women feel entitled to get compensated every month from her ex-husband, in order to pay her bills and rent, and other expenses that she spends on herself in order to attract the next victim (the next man) in her life to use and take advantage of. In other words, women cannot remarry and receive alimony, but she still can remain single or be in a secretive relationship with another man, and never be able to report her behavior to the court (and she never will) because she would be at risk of losing her benefits. So, this gives her a "Receive alimony pass" because this woman is still struggling to find work and "find the skills necessary in order to work" as this article implies and confirms. The feminist ideology is that women should be and are independent! This clearly cannot be the case, if women are consistently lining up at their court jurisdiction demanding alimony payments every month and for years, for allegedly being such a great wife and being vulnerable to the dangers of society once the marriage is obsolete. So if over 90% of women receive alimony, then we can understand why women desire marriage so much because they know within "their conscious" that they will benefit financially during marriage and once again financially once the marriage is obsolete (thanks to sexist and incompetent judges). In other words, it's a win/win situation for them. The whole reason for the typical American woman's excuse for getting married is that because "it's a little girl's dream" is the smaller excuse of a bigger reason and excuse to financially benefit themselves in any event that their initial/original career

Female Privileges in America!
Exposing Feminist Hypocrisy!

agenda fails on their end. If the author is so wrong, why is it that if 4 out of 10 American households which are women who are the ones who generate superior income than men, leave an alimony rate higher than men being eligible and accepted at a rate of only 3% when the divorces are settled? Certainly, it would be foolish to assume that 97% of men who did not qualify for alimony are because all of these men were abusive and unfaithful husbands. There are two reasons why men almost never receive alimony from women after the marriage is completely obsolete!

1. *Women are dependent, vindictive, vengeful, and claim to be delicate and vulnerable in a challenging world of employment which is allegedly (it's not really) biased against them. In other words, these women are incapable of being as superior as men in general therefore, they deserve special treatment for claiming to be the perfect wife during her marriage (she cooked, cleaned, took care of the children without day care assistance or maid assistance, and was always faithful to her husband and never lied to him).*
2. *Men have a pride within themselves (generally when they're married) to not beg or ask for alimony because it is unbecoming of a man who is determined to make himself responsible and prosperous with or without financial assistance from any resources and/or assistance from anyone else.*

Female Privileges in America!
Exposing Feminist Hypocrisy!

Note: In other words, men generally never waste their time seeking alimony because they have a mental belief of being "independent" which contradicts the average/typical female concept and conscious of "someone should pay my bills, take care of me, my children, and support my beliefs."

Indeed, today's mothers are the primary breadwinners in four out of 10 U.S. families, according to Pew Research. And though only 3% of the roughly 400,000 alimony recipients in 2010 were male, per Census data, the trend of spousal support awards from women to men is "definitely on the rise" as women's earnings continue to increase, New York divorce lawyer James Sexton told Moneyish.

Women have been responsible for paying spousal support since 1979, when the U.S. Supreme Court ruled in a landmark decision that alimony should be gender-neutral. Many states over the years have shifted away from permanent spousal support -- lifelong payments until death or the spouse's remarriage -- to alleviate the payer's burden and catch up with the modern marriage.

"The concept behind maintenance has evolved," Dilpreet Rai, a partner at the New York-based firm Hennessey and Bienstock LLP, told Moneyish. "Spousal support for a long duration is not as common as it (once was) ... It goes to the idea that it's about rehabilitation and getting someone back into the workforce, and making sure that they have time to get sufficient skills and training."

What's flawed about the alimony rate of at least 97% of women receiving alimony is that not only are the courts biased/sexist against men in favor of women, but also that women file, seek, and demand "alimony" more than men but this is a problem. If 40% of American households consist of women being the breadwinners of the family, and 97% of women are getting alimony, it's reasonable to assume that the breadwinners who are the 40% are still seeking alimony, and 97% of them are still getting alimony despite these women being the breadwinners. Because, if this was not the case, then women would only generally be receiving 60% of the time; which would be favorable alimony cases on their behalf. In other

Female Privileges in America!
Exposing Feminist Hypocrisy!

words, women work just like their husbands and maintain their children just as much as their husbands (in many cases), and still demand alimony because she "feels that she delivered more to the marriage than her husband." In other words, she is the victim and the husband is the perpetrator. She is entitled to compensation because she is the weaker sex (although she wants the court to believe in this theory with her complaints and arguements yet she will never admit it herself). However, the typical argument that women generally declare in their reasoning of refusing to be a "1950's wife" (which is to be loyal, faithful, cook, and clean and cater to her husband and her offspring) is that it's demeaning to them and inferior to them and "men have two hands and should do it himself; and also that women aren't taking men's crap anymore." This is the feminist argument and ideology. The reason why marriages fail is that men cheat and are abusive and desire to control women according to feminist and delusional women. However, after taking a closer look at the reasons why the divorce rates are common and happen in the United States, thanks to the confirmation source of the United States Census Bureau and worldpopulationreview.com, we will be able to understand the three reasons on why divorces generally occur.

Female Privileges in America!
Exposing Feminist Hypocrisy!

The average age for couples going through their first divorce is 30 years old. Couples are more or less likely to get divorced based on several factors. Couples married between the ages of 20-25 are 60% likely to get a divorce. Those who wait until they are older than 25 to get married are 24% less likely to get divorced. Those with strong religious beliefs are 14% less likely to get a divorce. The higher attainment of education someone has, the lower their risk of divorce is.

According to a U.S. Census Bureau survey, the top three reasons for divorces are incompatibility (43%), infidelity (28%), and money issues (22%).

So according to this article, divorces happen in the United States because of these three primary reasons:

1. *Incompatibility (It's no secret that women desire to change and manipulate a man before and after marriage to mold him into her liking and desires and sometimes this never works). Men do not seek to change women. Women seek to change men and for that reason alone, when women realize that their men will not change at all, they seek divorce and blame (almost always) everything on the man because he would not "step up to the plate" even though the woman selected this man to be with, marry, and probably breed with. It's all her fault. She picked him and refuses to take responsibility for her actions. Of course, the 43% of reasoning behind this, is that women are filing for divorce to begin with these reasons; unless of course, it's necessary to escape an abusive relationship from a man who beats and abuses her which is not the typical and primary reason for divorce at least according to these statistics.*

Female Privileges in America!
Exposing Feminist Hypocrisy!

2. *Infidelity became the second reason for divorces in the United States. This is very critical because for centuries and decades, men have earned the reputation of cheating more than women in relationships, but in the 21st century, women are gaining a popular reputation for being unfaithful and engaging in infidelity thanks to her actions, that she takes advantage of through social media. The truth is, women will never tell their son's this! Women cheat for money, sex, and love, and revenge! Men only cheat for sex! Those are the facts! What does this mean? Women are 4x more likely to cheat on their partner/spouse more than men since they almost always have the advantage to cheat.*

3. *Money issues are an issue because the economy! let's face it, these current circumstances were not designed in our current times to benefit millennials, and/or future younger generations when compared to earlier and older generations. Yes, these older generations destroyed our economy up on purpose to only benefit themselves. That was no accident! Looking forward, however, generally, American women desire luxury, clothes, bills paid on their behalf, special treatment (doors held open for them) among other things so when a man is struggling with financial difficulty, a woman will feel entitled and determined to seek another man to pay her bills and spoil her (as if she's an English queen) as she desires and as she falsely believes that she is entitled to. You don't believe the author? How many beautiful and thin-fit women do you see homeless*

Female Privileges in America!
Exposing Feminist Hypocrisy!

compared to handsome yet homeless men? (the author is not gay too by the way, he's just trying to make a point) When will you ever see a female who looks or resembles a model to be begging for money and/or food on the streets? Never! You will see plenty of men who could potentially be models that are homeless, but never women. If men are the primary breadwinners in families, and divorces happen because of this, it's not because the man who cannot pay for his wife's luxuries lines up in court, and demands to be divorced to request alimony from his wife. It's the opposite. The wife had expectations and those expectations were not met. So, she wants to end the divorce, quit, and give up easily like almost all women do in all of their professions when pressure and influence (from friends and family) gets to these women. Yet, these quitters demand equality and benefits; yet seek independence. The hypocrisy speaks for itself!

Now, we have talked about the subjects of marriage, and the reason behind all of these divorce actions engaged by women! However, this does not explain the reason why lesbian women divorce at a higher rate than gay married men? Allegedly, straight women are fed up with men's controlling/abusive actions as the reasoning for their decision to seek a divorce, however can the same excuse be applied towards gay women?

Here is the article of the divorce rate in the United States of same-sex couples being credited to at least on their published

Female Privileges in America!
Exposing Feminist Hypocrisy!

website www.reinherzlaw.com. Thanks for confirming my suspicion and facts!

It is unclear as to why the lesbian couples in this and other studies have gotten divorced at a higher rate than has been true of homosexual males: the top reason given for splitting was "unreasonable behavior," which is the UK's version of irreconcilable differences. Some sociologists have posited the notion that the women rushed into marriage with higher expectations and a greater sense of romance about the union than the more clear-eyed approach that the men had taken, but that theory has raised some eyebrows and objections. In Britain, lesbian couples were found to break up twice as frequently as gay men even before same-sex marriage became legal. A similar trend appeared in a study conducted on civil partnerships in Norway, Sweden and Denmark by researchers at Stockholm University.

It is interesting to note that even in heterosexual marriages, women are more likely to initiate a divorce than men are, and that may provide the most significant clue of all as to why the divorce rates are higher for lesbians than for gay men. Women may simply demand more from the relationship, or be quicker to acknowledge when it is no longer working.

Apparently to this article, gay women, like straight women, all around the world, who accept gay marriage are prone and desire to divorce at a much higer rate than heterosexual or homosexual men. According to this article, "it is unclear why this happens!" But the author knows why this happens and so do many rational-thinking people! Just like in heterosexual marriages, women are prone and likely to give up, quit, and run away from their problems more than men; and desire; and demand either their relatives or their local govenrnment to assist them with their financial needs because they're either sad, hurt, emotional, and cannot deal with their crisis in their

Female Privileges in America!
Exposing Feminist Hypocrisy!

marriage or all of these above reasons. I find it hard to believe that lesbian women are physically abusive more to their girlfriends than straight women are to their men, or straight men are to their women. Gay men, like straight men, don't desire to quit or give up on something so easily like women do because the truth is, women's mentality is weak and inferior. It's sad because many of these same women are in powerful positions and enter politics, and do nothing for their constituents or to change the world to make make their names in history. If you think that the author is wrong, look at the current women politicians representing the United States and/or other countries and see how popular their ratings are currently at the moment. These American women are in power and do nothing to make a positive legacy for themselves which is utterly embarrassing to women who desire true change and prosperity (the feminists who do nothing but complain about everything). It's sad that only men have delivered this with the exception of Queen Elizabeth I (not the second and current queen) to her country (England) who made England the golden age during her time. In other words, women can change history for the better, but never desire to do so! They only desire to benefit themselves and take advantage of innocent people. It should be noted that Queen Elizabaeth I never had children or was married and yet during her tenure, England benefited the most because she was dedicated to do to her job as a Queen of a then-super-nation unlike modern American women and other non-American women today who are only dedicated to benefit themselves and never make a name or

Female Privileges in America!
Exposing Feminist Hypocrisy!

mark a name for themselves in history. Prove the author wrong about this!

If men were so abusive and unfaithful, then why don't these same abusive married men file for divorce more than their alleged abused wife's? Let the ignorant and idiotic feminist answer this question on why her own species desires to give up, quit, and claim to be independent yet demand financial support from their previous partners and benefit themselves thanks to biased courts who are sexist against men and will continue to be; and the reason why people may ask these questions are these!

1. *Most of the judges in the courts are primarily men and are either silent generation or baby boomer Americans, which in their times, their current wives cooked, cleaned, and were loyal to them in addition to having a mother supporting their every move and decision. In other words, how could these men in courts find any flaw in women of any decade? Since women (from their generation) treated them with dignity and support? The reason is that these sorry ass judges cannot see the evil and the flawed characteristics of women since women (in their time and current status) have treated them (these older generation men) with respect and dignity. In other words, these judges are blind and prejudiced against older and younger men because these judges can never see the potential opportunity of women using, taking advantage and/or abusing men in general circumstances. No, it can't be possible! In these judges'*

Female Privileges in America!
Exposing Feminist Hypocrisy!

eyes, all women are innocent beyond a reasonable doubt. I'm not convinced however, that if millenial men were judges today, that the same opportunities would be granted to women, since millenial women are completely different from silent generation and baby boomer women. Millenial women desire special status but don't want to earn it unlike their mothers and grandmothers. That's a fact! The author is a millennial and has dated multiple women who are millennials and have met with other millenial women who believe in this "entitled concept." There may be an exception to this rule; however, this does not exclude the overwhelming millennial American women population. Again, prove the author wrong, with both millennial men (who analyze millennial women) and their actions and mentalities! Is the author wrong about this?

2. *Women only get married to benefit themselves. What does this mean? Like in the animal species, a lion will hunt for deer or a giraffe. Women do the same thing with men, but the only difference is that women use "financial advantages" rather than "killing advantages" against men in order to fulfill their agenda. For example, women will give sex to men, in all various sex positions, and give men all three of their holes (oral, vaginal & anal sex), while also cooooking and cleaning for him, but once the boyfriend, walks down the aisle with her and signs on that dotted line on a "contract of marriage" then it's all over for the man. It's very common at this point for women, once they get married*

Female Privileges in America!
Exposing Feminist Hypocrisy!

to get obese, cut their hair short, and engage in at least (or less) 50% less of household chores, and for some reason (because she's now married and can get alimony if her husband is defensive or questions her on her bullshit) are less resistant on criticizing her husband. The wife finds every reason and way to look for something that the husband does something wrong and hence, she intentionally disrupts the peaceful marriage with a nagging mentality (and sometimes physical) and abusive nature. Why don't men report this abuse to the police? It's the same reason why most men don't line up in court to demand alimony as much as women do! The reason for this is because it emasculates men, and men are generally too proud (in many circumstances) to quiver in fear, and demand to be compensated and/or treated because they are the victim of mental and physical abuse. The truth is, women abuse men mentally and physically all the time, but because of their gender, and their lies, law enforcement (and the judicial system) almost always believes their story and favors them regarding domestic violence cases. That needs to stop and men should report more mental and physical abuse demonstrated against them by women, who claim equality, but still in their conscious desire "special treatment." I believe that if men properly reported this abuse and acted against them, then the domestic violence reports geared towards women would significantly increase but may be less than men abusing women. However, women should not get a "free ride of

Female Privileges in America!
Exposing Feminist Hypocrisy!

abuse" just because of their gender. This is definite special treatment geard in favor of women against men when women can be and may be as often as the main culprit of crimes regarding domestic violence cases. Is the author wrong about this?

3. *Isn't it strange that feminist women rally, request and demand equal treatment, equal pay, and equal opportunities for women and yet they never stand in line to protest to "end all spousal support" even though these same "unpatriotic women" know that women receive almost always in their favor because of their gender and "victim status" spousal support? If a woman is receiving spousal support, then she cannot be "independent" and contradicts that feminist concept and mentality. If wealthy women who have everything in life, that a poor woman can never obtain or has never experienced in her life, continue to collect "spousal support" from their ex-husband than that woman (in these rare cisrumstances) may be independent but out of being vindictive is still convincing herself that she is entitled to receive spousal support, for her service to her husband which was primarily sex, some cooking, and some cleaning and taking care of their kids. If feminists are so equal to men, why don't they ever protest against spousal support? What if a woman is not a feminist, and she still decides never to protest against spousal support? The reason why is because these women (desire and crave an insurance policy on their behalf in case the marriage does not work out in their favor and*

Female Privileges in America!
Exposing Feminist Hypocrisy!

that eventually after divorce proceedings, these women have to find work to get their hands dirty which they will never want or ever intended to do or expect and almost always will refuse) cannot come up with a back up plan for their failed marriage (which they probably failed themselves since women are generally the ones to file for divorce compared to men) because American women know that they have a time clock set on them which inevitably expires. Once these women reach an old age, or an age that men are not impressed with, (which is typically 32 years of age and above for women), American men desire not to seek interest in these women, because these women come with baggage, problems, and generally never reciprocate anything meaningful towards the relationship. These women take up all kinds of resources (Money, property & time), but never supply these resources back in return towards men. If the author is so wrong, when do you ever hear of women (of all ages and generations) purchasing a home or a car for their boyfriend/husband? Yet, how many times have there been stories of men purchasing houses and cars for women? That's the whole point! American women are cheap and are already programmed to take, but never to give back, and if she does, it's a very small portion of a donation, for which she expects almost always a greater value of that donation in return. Men are more generous by nature and women are more selfish by nature! American women have this engineered mentality of taking, taking, accepting, but never giving,

Female Privileges in America!
Exposing Feminist Hypocrisy!

giving, giving; and to American women, sex is the ultimate reward to men in return of all the financial support and assistance that men render towards their women. What's hypocritical about this is that women use sex as a way to influence men and trap a man because in her mind she thinks that this is to install a man's wants and desires; yet she also enjoys the pleasurable sex experiences even if the man is bad in bed; the woman still enjoys a moment of intimate sex; which means that women receive more benefits (sex, money, homes, cars, opportunities) than men who have no choice but to have to work for the rest of their lives to establish a decent income in order to pay their bills and their agenda(s) whatever those agendas may be.

4. *Have you ever heard that phrase that a wealthy man (entrepreneur, actor, politician) can change a poor woman's life (maid, cook, hairdresser) and a wealthy woman (entrepreneur, actor, politician) can never change a poor man's life? The reason for this is because men can and will never care generally about how much a woman is intelligent or makes in terms of income unless the man is lazy, entitled, a socialist, and has no ambition or pride to do anything with his life. In other words, a wealthy man does not mind dating and supporting a beautiful poor woman who probably works as a server at a restaurant, and has nothing to her name in terms of any financial value. She may have baggage (debt and/or kids), and men may take on these many responsibilities. However, when do you ever hear of a*

Female Privileges in America!
Exposing Feminist Hypocrisy!

wealthy woman ever dating a male dishwasher or janitor who works at a restaurant or warehouse? The answer is never! Why? Because even wealthy women (like the average lower and middle class American women) are selfish and desire never to compensate anyone or transition a poor man (to a wealthy man) to pay all of his requested extravagant expenses, because the typical American woman never desires to be a "sugar mama" and yet has no problem seeking "sugar daddies" who will pay for all of her extravagant expenses." Again, prove the author wrong about this!

Note: To all men, reading this, save yourself the problems, headaches, biasness from courts, financial obligations, and other requirements from getting married. You will never win in marriage! A very small percentage of men win monetary avantages, circumstances, and positive reputations after getting a divorce, which is only 3% (so much for men's rights). There will never be a benefit to a responsible and hard-working man to get married. Here are the reasons on why a man should never get married to his girlfriend no matter how great she is in bed, and no matter how much she is willing to contribute towards rent, utilities, bills, and cooking, and cleaning (if she does which many American women today do not engage in many if not all of these practices)

1. *Men will always lose (economically) in almost all cases of divorces regardless if the man filed first for divorce first, or if the woman was unfaithful. Women always win,*

Female Privileges in America!
Exposing Feminist Hypocrisy!

because even though the courts declare "equality" for all genders, races, and people in general they certainly do not practice it with their actions. These people are lawyers and employed by their local, state, and federal governments so they easily get away with their behavior. After all, how could a judge ever be accused of being impractical and biased? Well, in the United States, this does happen. Again, prove the author wrong in this that for every man reading this paragraph and currently has to pay alimony to an unfaithful woman who complained to the courts and convinced the judge of her being innocent, was so easily protected, and her husband was punished for his innocence. It's fair to say that these old ass judges are pussy whipped themselves and for those female judges, they know how women are, but are in favor of their own species because they're prejudiced against men, which is not all female judges in the United States of America, but the majority of them in the United States. If the author is wrong about these accusations, then why don't any female judges ever do anything to benefit men's circumstances more financially and/or equally when comparing them to women's circumstances? It's never going to happen because women are only hellbent on helping themselves and their own species. Generally, this is how the majority of American women are.
2. *We've already covered why men should not get married because if his wife is unhappy, she can easily cry (and crawl) her ass to the court and beg the judge for a*

Female Privileges in America!
Exposing Feminist Hypocrisy!

divorce and alimony. More than likely, she will get what she asks for and feels entitled too even though in many cases she did not earn it. This is just a sample and a portion of what women receive after a divorce. It depends on many factors and circumstances; depending on what assets the man has, and if the woman demands those assets. Here is a list of things that generally women receive after a divorce:
Note: I'm not including child support because that topic is specifically reserved for the next incoming chapter (III).

- *Houses/residences/condos/vacation homes/apartments and/or motorhomes.*
- *Automobiles of every kind (even if it's her husband's motorcycle which she demands to receive even though she would never use or operate the motorcycle itself but only out of being vindictive against her husband she will demand the motorcycle)*
- *Furniture of various elegant and expensive values.*
- *Appliances of any kind (refrigerators, washer/dryers, air conditioners, microwaves, toasters, and/or coffeemakers).*
- *Business assets or ownership in a business that her husband started without any assistance from her whatsoever.*
- *Entertainment centers (televisions, gaming equipment, DVD/Blu-Ray players, computers, cell phones, internet modems/routers, antennas, cable boxes, and/or Ipods).*

Female Privileges in America!
Exposing Feminist Hypocrisy!

- *Anything that may not be valuable towards the woman, but knows that her ex-husband will enjoy having it's comfort in his possession, so she will do everything that she can to beg the judge to own this property just to take it away from him as an act of being spiteful. It's not that she wants this item or desires to give it away and sell it, she just wants to take away anything that can make her ex-husband comfortable and satisfied. It's pretty much the idea of a person being childish, and women can get away with this, and very rarely can men get away with this same typical behavior that women commonly engage in. It's sad and pathetic; but the only alternative to avoid this from happening to you men out there, is to never waste your time, money, effort, and/or savings to purchase a ring for your potential future ex-wife who is currently your girlfriend. The sex is not worth it and her pussy is not made of gold, no matter how much she thinks, acts, and wakes up every day in the morning to believe in that nonsense.*

3. Getting married to a woman never can or will guarantee you a lifetime partner where you grow old together and die together. Women want to believe in this fantasy and in many cases attempt to manipulate their men with this fantasy, because of their grandparents who are still married and have been married for several decades, but these same women don't want to do all of the same household chores, responsibilities, and/or efforts to make a marriage work like their grandmothers did in their decades and time. Their

Female Privileges in America!
Exposing Feminist Hypocrisy!

grandmothers did not pop frozen-food-products in the microwave for her husband to eat because she refused to cook, or was too lazy to cook, or did not know how to cook, or because she felt that "cooking is inferior to women like modern women believe it to be." In other words, these modern women, which are typically liberal women, and the younger generation women, want the benefits of treatment like their grandmothers received through their hard working effort to please and satisfy their men, but do not want the responsibilities. Modern American women expect men to be traditional today, but refuse to be traditional themselves today. As a result of this typical and common behavior by American women, men should not expect to live "happily ever after" with a woman because there is no guarantee that the woman can make him happy. There is no guarantee that she will stay loyal, faithful, nurturing, affectionate, sexually active with you (but not with other people), and there is no guarantee that she will also not be in the future (if she isn't already) mentally and physically abusive towards you. This is very important men, because if a woman strikes you first during an argument, and you push her back, regardless if you call the police first, you will be the one arrested (generally) once law enforcement arrives to question you and your girlfriend or wife and while you're being booked in jail, she will be able to remain inside your residence, and while she has access to all of your belongings and can do as she pleases with them, do not expect some of your personal merchandise to disappear and/or be destroyed while you're freezing in jail and smelling other peoples farts. You have no say in anything. If it's a battery

Female Privileges in America!
Exposing Feminist Hypocrisy!

charge that you have been charged with by your local police department, depending on the state where you live in, here are the general and common deprivation of civil liberties that you will endure and face (for several years) even if you know in your heart that you're innocent. Karma will not save you or your religion no matter how much that you pray. Prove the author wrong about this!

- *If convicted of domestic violence against your wife (even if she was your girlfriend), you will lose your gun rights for years or for life; even if it's just an automatic temporary restraining order given to your wife with or without her consent because a domestic violence charge is a mandatory requirement for the courts to issue one for her against you. Even if you're never convicted, or in the process of your trial you will have to surrender your gun of any kind to your local police station. If you're convicted in the State of California for example, of domestic violence, your second amendment right is terminated for a minimum of ten years. There is no way to overturn this gun-ban unless of course you can somehow prove to your local police department and the courts with an appeal that you were innocent. No matter how much you enjoy duck hunting, or shooting at beer cans, you can not own a gun for ten years. That's the law at least in the current author's state. If you're thinking that "hey it's okay, I don't want a gun or need a gun anyway, or it's okay, I'll just wait ten years to get a gun, forget it!"*

Female Privileges in America!
Exposing Feminist Hypocrisy!

- *According to this law enforcement website, "legislation/policy on www.atf.gov" thanks to the constitution-hating-politicians, a domestic violence conviction to a man is a guaranteed firearm ban for him no matter how many years and decades pass him. You're right to own a gun is obsolete! Additionally, if you think that getting your domestic violence record expunged will return your right to own a firearm, that depends on a few factors. It depends on which jurisdiction that you reside in and if the judge will grant you this permission. The courts do not care how much of a law-abiding citizen that you have been or how much taxes you pay to your city, state, and federal government. Being convicted of domestic violence pretty much labels you the greatest piece of shit in the eyes of the court after a pedophile and a rapist. Prove the author wrong about this!*

Female Privileges in America!
Exposing Feminist Hypocrisy!

MISDEMEANOR CRIMES OF DOMESTIC VIOLENCE AND FEDERAL FIREARMS PROHIBITIONS

Persons who have been convicted in any court of a qualifying misdemeanor crime of domestic violence (MCDV) generally are prohibited under Federal law from possessing any firearm or ammunition in or affecting commerce (or shipping or transporting any firearm or ammunition in interstate or foreign commerce, or receiving any such firearm or ammunition). This prohibition also applies to federal, state, and local governmental employees in both their official and private capacities. Violation of this prohibition is a federal offense punishable by up to ten years imprisonment. See Title 18 U.S.C. § 922(g)(9) (the Lautenberg Amendment), see also 18 U.S.C. §§ 921(a)(33), 924(a)(2), 925(a)(1), 27 C.F.R. §§ 478.11, 478.32.

A qualifying MCDV is an offense that:

- Is a federal, state, local, tribal or territorial offense that is a misdemeanor under federal, state or tribal law;
- Has the element of the use or attempted use of physical force, or the threatened use of a deadly weapon; and,
- At the time the offense was committed, the defendant was:
  - A current or former spouse, parent, or guardian of the victim;
  - A person with whom the victim shared a child in common;
  - A person who was cohabiting with or had cohabited with the victim as a spouse, parent, or guardian; or,
  - A person who was or had been similarly situated to a spouse, parent, or guardian of the victim.

Affirmative defenses/EXCEPTIONS: A person has not been convicted of a qualifying MCDV:

- IF the person was not represented by counsel — unless he or she knowingly and intelligently waived the right to counsel;
- IF the person was entitled to a jury trial AND the case was not tried by a jury — unless the person knowingly and intelligently waived the right to jury trial; or,
- IF the conviction was set aside or expunged; the person was pardoned; or, the person's civil rights – the right to vote, sit on a jury, and hold elected office – were restored (if the law of the applicable jurisdiction provides for the loss of civil rights under such an offense).

BUT: This exception does NOT lift the federal firearms prohibition if:

- the expungement, pardon, or restoration of civil rights expressly provides that the person may not ship, transport, possess, or receive firearms; or,
- the person is otherwise prohibited by the law of the jurisdiction in which the proceedings were held from receiving or possessing any firearms.

- *The fact of the matter is that men are better off living alone and in separate residences from their current*

Female Privileges in America!
Exposing Feminist Hypocrisy!

girlfriends who anticipate getting a proposal from their boyfriends.

To save yourself (the man) the pain, agony, and headaches from typical American women, it's better to live alone, be alone, and act alone. Women try to manipulate and deceive men with a false notion and belief "that if men don't get married and settle down, they will die in misery and alone with no one on their side; and because of this, they will miss out on a great opportunity." The truth is, very few American women give American men great opportunities and actually make them happy. Also, men will not generally die alone as they generally have friends, family, servants (butlers & maids), animals and other people to frequently communicate with them. Speaking of animals, it's really sad how a cat or a dog will always be loyal and faithful to its male owner, than the average typical American woman who is always ready and motivated to lie, cheat, and/or betray her man to benefit herself. In other words, sometimes it's better to have an animal by your side than the average typical American woman. Prove the author wrong about this!

The only pre-benefit that a man can receive prior to getting married is the right to ask his ex-girlfriend back the engagement ring that he purchased for. Some women agree to give the ring back, but many women fight tooth and nail (sometimes literally) and legally not to return the ring back. This only proves the fact that marriage is a contract for both men and women. The reason why is because most states in the United States require the woman (or the person) to return the

Female Privileges in America!
Exposing Feminist Hypocrisy!

ring back regardless if the man or woman or person decided to terminate the engagement. In the eyes of the court, an engagement ring is a "conditional gift" that is given to a person in return for a service, payment, and/or agreement. In this case, the marriage was the agreement. It certainly can't be a service to a man, because the man doesn't get any service whatsoever from getting married to a woman since many women don't want to cook, clean, or do anything remotely beneficial towards their man after getting married yet alone before getting married. Marriage can be a payment in return to the man but this usually involves illegal immigration circumstances, which is a woman paying a man to marry her in order for her to receive proper documentation to reside in the United States inevitably long enough for her to become a citizen (the author was offered $10,000 USD dollars to marry a Salvadorean women but refused the offer despite her being sexy and attractive. Most ordinary American women, as it is, generally like to never pay for any expenses and rely and expect the man to pay her expenses of all artifacts, bills, and objects prior to the marriage, so you can imagine that American women will hardly or never pay anything to her boyfriend in order to get married. What is the last option left in this? An agreement! There are a handful of states (Alaska, Alabama, Kentucky, Massachusetts, and New Hampshire) that still legally allow the woman to keep the ring even if the man cancels the engagement. It's bullshit but that's the way it is. Montana is the only pussy-whipped state that allows a woman to keep the ring; even if it's an unconditional gift regardless if the engagement is cancelled.

Female Privileges in America!
Exposing Feminist Hypocrisy!

Note: This comes to my next point, if any man ever wants to ignore my warnings on never getting married, then at least never give an engagement ring to your girlfriend on her birthday as a surprise! Why? Because, in any event your ex-girlfriend won't voluntarily give you the engagement ring back and now you have to take her to court for her refusal to not give you back the ring that your entitled to; and her argument for keeping the ring to the judge can be that the engagement ring was a gift on her birthday, or she will bullshit the judge and say that it was an ordinary promise ring and use this as her argument to keep the engagement ring because promise rings are "unconditional gifts" no matter how much it's value is. Engagement rings are generally "conditional gifts." In the current state of California, (surprisingly), the man gets the ring back but only after proof that he shows to the judge that the ring was indeed given in return for a marriage. That would be an engagement and a proposal that was agreed upon between both parties yet somehow cancelled. If you're thinking on buying the engagement ring, It would be great and to your benefit to also ask the cashier to title your receipt manually through and-writing or typing (if the product which is the engagement ring only states "diamond ring") to ensure that you can prove to the courts that the ring that you purchased is indeed an engagement ring and not any other ring. However, to avoid all of this nonsense and headaches, just don't buy the fucking ring in the first place. Believe me, if you think about all the wrong things that your current girlfriend has done towards you versus the right things that she

Female Privileges in America!
Exposing Feminist Hypocrisy!

has done geared towards you, you can determine and analyze if she's worth settling down and marrying. Treat every woman that you meet like a scale and see if she's balanced or if the "good qualities" outweighs the "bad qualities." It's very hard to find a girl in the United States that outweighs bad characteristics with good characteristics. Use your insticnt and common sense men. This can potentially save you thousands if not millions of dollars for you!

4. Being convicted of a domestic violence charge, doesn't just take away a man's right to own guns. It also makes it harder for him to find stable employment with all of the many background checks that employers do these days on candidates who seek positions with their companies. Believe me, the job rejections working for almost any position for your metropolitan city, or any corporate position, or even a grave-digger at your local cemetery will deny you the right to work because of your record regardless of your qualifications, experiences, and licenses. In other words, "once guilty, always guilty." Unless you get your record expunged, with a domestic violence record on your behalf, you will unlikely be able to rent an apartment/house/condo, find stable employment, join the military in all branches because you can't own a firearm, hence you're not allowed to practice with one either (even if it's front of government employees to help protect national security), become a police officer, firefighter, or secret service agent protecting the president of the United States. You can run for president and get elected president of the United States with a domestic violence record, which is ass backwards when

Female Privileges in America!
Exposing Feminist Hypocrisy!

the requirements to run for president does not limit anyone because of their criminal history; but law enforcement does, even though the president is in charge of the military. You get the point though. Domestic violence charges usually happen after a physical dispute between a couple. In many cases, women provoke these circumstances and are never held accountable. To avoid these potential circumstances from happening to you, don't ever live with a woman, and don't ever get married. Believe me, you will almost always lose when something happens bad between both of you. Your career, your agenda, your future is not worth it to any American woman out there. What matters is that you focus on yourself and your dreams. Women are dream killers by nature. Almost never, do women ever assist or encourage their man to follow his dreams unless she knows that she's compensated for it in some way. She never does anything for free. Again, to avoid useless and worthless women in your life and like drugs, just say no to both of them! Both can destroy your life permanently. For now, let's move on to chapter 3 to prove more female privilege in America, if this chapter has not convinced you (the reader) yet of all the benefits and opportunities that women receive and get away with compared to men for the same opportunities/benefits.

III

Female Privileges in America!
Exposing Feminist Hypocrisy!

-Child Support & Custody-

This chapter will piss off both men and women. This chapter will piss off men because of facts and discrepancies within their court jurisdiction and other facts regarding other court jurisdictions. This chapter will also piss off women because this chapter exposes the truth about American women who are so quick to collect child support, but refuse to pay child support to men which is challenging every opportunity to give men compensation who are watching, providing, and taking care of his offspring; and therefore, cannot stand the fact that the father of their child is involved because the woman (who is the mother) has a difficult time and experience convincing her son or daughter that the father is a deadbeat and does not care for his offspring. The mother's credibility cannot be accepted or believed if the father is in the picture; no matter how much the ex-girlfriend, ex-wife, or fiance tries to manipulate her child to believe in this alleged false accusation regarding her father's welfare beliefs geared towards his own daughter. In other words, the father has an alibi and an ultimate defense and excuse on why he is not 100% involved in his own offspring's activities. The truth is, women act like cowards and shield themselves with their own children to attack the father of her child not necessarily because he's a bad father, but because he may have been a bad boyfriend or husband. Women are spiteful and vindictive in this behavior. You may ask yourself, "what is their method or way of being vindictive?" Well, a father could be a great father and the

Female Privileges in America!
Exposing Feminist Hypocrisy!

mother of that same child; and yet the mother can and will always use the typical excuse of telling her son and/or daughter the following false accusations:

- *"If your father cared about you, he would spend more time with you!"*
- *"Your father cares more about women than he does about you, which is why you should trust me and never trust him!"*
- *"Your father cheated on me and betrayed me, therefore, he can easily betray you and lie to you and he will because he's a dog!"*
- *"Look at your friends father's and how much they spend time with their children when compared to your father who is always working and never takes time off to see you!"*

Did you read these four typical and common statements given by single (resentful) women who are allegedly educated and attempting to manipulate the father's offspring about their own biological father refusing to be a part of his or her life through these false accusations? While it may be true about certain father's who are useless and desire not to be a part of his son's life or his daughter's life, this is truly a small percentage. Most fathers, whether married or single, desire or attempt to be a part of his or her daughters life. However, the greatest obstacle in the single father's path is not only the courts, it's his ex-wife or ex-girlfriend. Just like domestic violence cases, alimony cases, and any other cases favoring women, any man reading

Female Privileges in America!
Exposing Feminist Hypocrisy!

this paragraph should believe that men generally will never win against women when it comes to child custody and/or child support cases. Since women earn less than men (because they refuse to do dangerous jobs as men that pay more), they're entitled to receive not only child support but also child custody because these women gave birth to these children and therefore they're entitled to keep them.

So much for the angry, typical woman's argument on how it takes two people (a man and a woman) to make a child when that woman demands and expects child support in regards to child support payments; but when it comes to child custody it's a different case. Women feel privileged and entitled to keep her child but not privileged and entitled to refuse child support which more than likely does not go to her child or children but rather to herself! Neither do women feel privileged and entitled to pay child support to men who earn less than the mother and/or is a much more responsible parent than the mother who may have a typical reputation of being lazy, unwilling to cook, clean, and be motherly or contribute towards parental duties that is necessary in order to raise a child in general. Here is a graph of the percentage of men currently paying child support when in comparison to women. Again, if women are inferior to men in "the eyes of the court" then why don't they generally pay child support in at least 85% of child support cases to men like men do to women? The reason why is because the courts generally favor women and grant them their every wish and desire which is another reason to caution never to breed with certain American women yet

Female Privileges in America!
Exposing Feminist Hypocrisy!

alone marry them unless of course the world is underpopulated and in addition the courts are equal towards men regarding judgements which in either case will never happen in the United States (not at least in our lifetime)! Courts realize that women bitch, demand, complain, request, demand and expect special treatment regarding civil cases in addition to every other case that requires a hearing from a biased judge. However, never will the judges report this behavior from women to the media or write about this behavior in a book or declare these accurate accusations to a filmmaker who desires to make a film about "women's rights" and speak on behalf of their voices. Why? You might ask? Like politicians, judges are opportunists and only care about their own reputation, pensions, compensation, and elections like almost all politicians. They could care less about the truth, because judges are sexist and biased by their profession. If they speak about women wasting the courts time (and they do) and take advantage of women, it would possibly not only destroy the reputation of the judge (because the media will challenge automatically his or her accusations) but it may also destroy the reputation of one of the three branch of governments which is "the judicial branch." As it is, and I believe most people reading this paragraph can agree that the judicial branch is already corrupt and opportunistic. Like career politicians who generally exist (and do nothing useful in our states and the entire United States in regards to economic advantages and circumstances towards their constituents), we also have the same thing with "career judges" who do nothing but favor

Female Privileges in America!
Exposing Feminist Hypocrisy!

women's arguments always even when they're wrong against men's arguments against them!

Dads Represent 85% Of Child Support Providers, Pay More Than Female Payers

By Nathan Arnold

Special to DadsDivorce.com

Dads continue to pay child support payments more often and in larger amounts than mothers, according to new statistics on child support providers and payments released by the U.S. Census Bureau.

Men account for 85% of those ordered to pay child support.

Even in the rare instance where the mother is ordered to pay child support, courts are not ordering women to pay as much as male providers. Annual child support payments averaged $5,450 from male providers and $3,500 from female providers, nearly 56% less.

Overall, child support payments averaged $5,150 annually, or $430 per month.

According to the report, 59% of the $41.7 billion ($24.4 billion) in total payments from support providers were for child support for children under 21, paid by 4.8 million parents. The remaining amount was support paid to children over 21, parents, and other adults not living in the provider's household.

Visit the U.S. Census Bureau website for complete child support statistics.

Since the liberal left-socialist-feminists women always believe and support the media (except fox news) and their government, let us not give credibility to this article because after all, this journalist is part of the media and would never lie on behalf of the American people! However, these useless liberal women do not get to pick and choose. After carefully reading and understanding this article (by a truthful-competent man Nathan Arnold), we can begin to understand that women in the United States (generally) are not independent, will never be independent, and can never achieve the status of being independent (like men) because of their personal decisions that

Female Privileges in America!
Exposing Feminist Hypocrisy!

they make for themselves. For example, if this article is accurate that men are paying 85% of child support towards their offspring, then this would imply and confirm the notion that women are dependent on men and in no way is there a fact that men are 85% of the time irresponsible fathers. As the author mentioned earlier in his book that women are so hell-bent and determined to take their men to court in order to divorce him; and take away any earnings that he rightfully deserves and has earned throughout his lifetime, but of course, the courts and his ex-wife think differently. She feels entitled to everything that you (the man has earned) including child support even if the fact that you spent more than 50% of the time, feeding, supporting, clothing, defending the child (from a mentally and abusive mother and other people), and even more important; taking care of your own offspring under all circumstances and from all oppositions and barriers from the mother of your child that she feels that she is entitled to practice and engage in because of her gender and her supreme belief of "entitlement." Since women give birth to children, and in the process of giving birth, she feels pain, bleeds, and gives new life on Earth, so she automatically generally feels that she should have top priority rights over her child more than the father. In other words, she acts as if she's the superior parent and will only stop recognizing this delusion when the father of her child wants either nothing to do with her and the child and/or refuses to pay a generous amount of child support even if the father is paying child support but not enough to properly compensate the child in order for the child to be well-nourished, well-fed, and properly being given resources

Female Privileges in America!
Exposing Feminist Hypocrisy!

and provisions. Only then, if the father of his child continues in any of these actions, does the mother somehow and magically acknowledge that the father is an equal parent to her because "it takes two to make a baby." But the mother would not believe in this "equal treatment or status of parents" if the father was paying a decent amount of child support or more than enough child support so the mother could spend that money on herself. Sadly, only when it does not benefit the woman's financial circumstances, does the father become recognized as a superior parent as equally as the mother. Prove me wrong in this! This newspaper article confirms several accuracies regarding women's entitled belief of obtaining child support because she more than likely victimized herself in front of the already-biased courts who seem to always side on behalf of women's arguments, and not because of what she argues about in court which is necessarily accurate, but because women lie just as much as men do (if not more) to get what they want and desire. Because, even though these women claim to be equal, the courts never treat them as inferior or equal but rather as a "superior status." Throughout this book, in later chapters, I will provide an overwhelming comparison of the crimes that both men and women engage in, and the consequences (the biased lenient sentencing that women receive compared to men for the same crime in a convicted status). For now, we will focus on child support. As this article states, that does not only describe the fact that women receive 85% of child support payments from the fathers of their children, but also that if the 15% population of women that are court-ordered to pay child support to men, obviously

Female Privileges in America!
Exposing Feminist Hypocrisy!

pay less in child support payments than the rest of the 85% of men who pay child support towards their children which would indicate that there is definitely inequality regarding child support between both genders. What does this mean exactly?

- *Courts give single mothers exclusive priority and benefits because of her gender and because in the eyes of the court she's an automatic victim.*
- *85% of single fathers are not given exclusive priority and benefits to their status as a parent because the courts accept and view men as being less capable of being a victim or being taken advantage of. Therefore the courts (the judges and attorneys) will never admit this in public with their words, but with their actions, they're able to get away with this behavior; on behalf of "so-called" independent women or at least who claim to be independent.*
- *The courts do not care how much the father has to pay for child support, so long as he pays the required amount, regardless if the father is homeless and/or struggles financially. To prove this point, it's really unacceptable and sexist against men for women to have to pay 56% less child support for their child if the father is receiving child support, than the man who has to pay 56% more towards the mother if he is the one ordered to pay child support by the courts. There's a big difference between men paying annually child support payments of $5,450 dollars to their children, than women paying in annual payments a lesser amount of $3,500 towards*

Female Privileges in America!
Exposing Feminist Hypocrisy!

child support payments. Now, ask yourself this? Is this fair? Do all of these single mothers or women who are in a relationship and who have children deserve 85% of the time child support?

Here's why these abusive laws are biased and sexist against men and for all of those delusional feminists reading this, and still claim to be treated unequally compared to men, here are the facts to remind you on how wrong, stupid, and ignorant you are!

1. *If women earn less money than men, because they refuse to do dangerous and more challenging jobs as men engage in on a frequent basis (which is their decision and choice), than obviously the courts will more than likely award the woman not only child custody and child support because, she does not work as often as the father does, and she earns less money because she feels entitled to work in a safe, privileged work environment which in these cases, unless you work in a corporate position, you will generally receive low wages for typical office work and duties including the medical field. In other words, women are being rewarded by the courts not necessarily for being the better, over nurturing, and responsible parent that the father is or could be, but because of her irresponsible choices and decisions that she made in her lifetime. Men don't get this opportunity because men have to work in both safe and dangerous occupations in order to sustain*

Female Privileges in America!
Exposing Feminist Hypocrisy!

themselves economically. It's either that or be homeless.
Prove me wrong!
2. *If 85% of women are receiving child support payments in the United States, that means that 85% of single mothers forced themselves to go to court and demand the courts to deliver child support payments from the father either because his current child support payments are not enough money for her and her child or children, or she wants more money for herself to spend (some mothers spend child support payments on themselves instead of spending it on their actual children) exclusively for herself, or she just wants to be vindictive and bleed the father dry of, as much financial resources from the single father that she can possibly get away with. There could be the other option or reason on dead-beat dads who contribute nothing towards his child or children, but again as much as this single father may be the lowest piece of shit oon the planet for not putting food into his own child or children's mouth, who's the one who picked this dead-beat father to breed with to begin with? It's the mother's fault because she chose to have a child with a dead-beat father. For her irresponsible choices yet again, the courts reward her for her foolish actions and entitled gender. The media and the feminist liberal delusional women either deliberately ignore these facts or they're ignorant themselves. There can't be a third option regarding these actions.*

Female Privileges in America!
Exposing Feminist Hypocrisy!

3. *The author is not against child support payments or child custody. However, more women should be paying child support and in an equal portion as men do, because single fathers are now taking on more responsibility than women do (work longer hours without taking time off work like women generally do), because modern women especially in the United States, and never before in the history in America, have women lost their children as much as they do today, due to negligence (refusing to cook, clean, and render attention to their children). As a result of this, single fathers are now having to work more, cook, clean, and take care of their children at a much higher rate today, because too many American women today feel entitled, privileged, and superior in her status that she is immune from responsibility. It's generally assumed that if women lose custody of their children and the father has 100% custody of the children, that would imply or indicate that the mother herself was a dead-beat or irresponsible parent, and/or incapable of taking care of her children's responsibility yet she was fully capable of breeding. The author happens to believe in this assumption.*
4. *If women are only paying 15% of child support to victorious fathers who were somehow either lucky or able to convince the judge that the mother "should be the one forking over money to him rather than him to her" is because she either is a dead-beat mom, financially irresponsible with her money (she spends it on herself), and/or because she makes more money than*

Female Privileges in America!
Exposing Feminist Hypocrisy!

him, and the judge was somehow convinced of this alleged conduct that's been practiced by the mother on a consistent basis. However, the author is convinced that in many cases, single fathers were able to provide overwhelming evidence to judges on how much of a "reckless spender" or "irresponsible and an abusive parent that the mother" was (and still is), and the judges felt compassion and sorrow for the mother because all she had to do was shed a few tears in court to convince the judge that she is the victim and therefore after being humiliated in court, this gives her an exclusive pass and opportunity to be rewarded by the judge any applicable benefits, and what will the judge do? The sexist judge will more than likely feel sorry for the single mother and side with her despite overwhelming evidence that proves beyond a reasonable doubt that she's a liar, an opportunist, a user, a manipulator, and her integrity has been challenged by facts by the single father and maybe her criminal background if she has one. The bad thing about courts for men, is that men have to provide pictures, videos, audio testimony in order for the courts to generally give him some or all credibility regarding child custody and child support payments. All women have to do is just speak their mind, and look pretty, and the already-biased judges who claim to represent "equality to everyone under the law" generally side with women. What's even more pathetic in this is that women don't even have to ask for "equal treatment under the law" because she already receives it

Female Privileges in America!
Exposing Feminist Hypocrisy!

automatically the moment that she generally enters the courtroom. It's not equal treatment either that she expects either; she expects and demands special and superior treatment in the same way that women expect men to hold open doors for them, such as women expect judges to "open the door" of opportunity for them to receive child support payments and child custody from the single father!

5. *Let this be a reminder to every reader and to every man reading this paragraph! If men fail to pay child support towards their children (regardless if he's broke or not or if the economy sucks), then they can be in contempt of court, and here are the following consequences/penalties that (depending on the state that the man resides in) generally men always receive from the already-biased courts against them.*

   - *Frozen bank accounts (this penalty doesn't make any sense because how is the father supposed to show proof that he is paying child support when all he can pay with is cash which has difficulty establishing any form of alibi or credibility. After all, the mother can always deny ever receiving any cash payments and the courts will more than likely believe her even if she's lying).*
   - *Suspended driver's license (this penalty also doesn't make any sense because reliable transportation increases any opportunity for a single father to properly attend his work-place*

Female Privileges in America!
Exposing Feminist Hypocrisy!

and therefore being able to make money and pay child support. If men are only allowed to walk and take public transportation to work, why don't dead-beat moms who owe child support payments to the father of their child ever have to walk their asses to work like alleged dead-beat dads)?

- *Suspending professional licenses (registered nurse license, accountant license, electrician license, real estate broker license, massage therapist license, hairdresser license, police officer certification and license, teacher licenses, and for those bartenders out there that owe child support, this also can include your liquor license). If you notice this penalty doesn't make any sense at all because all of these licenses convert directly and indirectly towards "generating revenue" which is what's needed in order to pay child support. That's the only reason why these people get licenses/certifications to begin with, which is to "make money" independently or work for an employer who hires employees conditionally so long as they possess the appropriate license and/or certification for their company, which again is for the employee to "make money." You can't pay child support, if you don't have money. This penalty also doesn't make sense either because if single mothers are struggling so bad with child support payments, wouldn't it be common sense to allow the dead-beat dads to*

Female Privileges in America!
Exposing Feminist Hypocrisy!

make more money with his license/certificate/credentials and then for the entitled single mother to cry and beg the courts for more money from the dead-beat dads since evidence suggests and reveals (at least according to the Bureau of Labor Statistics) that occupations that require licenses/certifications/credentials generally provide an "above average" income? **Prove me wrong about this!**

- *Reporting to the three tyrannical credit bureaus (Equifax, TransUnion, Experian) who dominate your life from the moment that you turn 18 years old, until the day that you're dead, if you owe child support and your credit report receives this notification, unless this record gets "disputed" or taken care (because you realize that you owe money), than this can potentially plummet and damage your credit score by dozens if not hundreds of points; regardless if you pay your bills on time and all of your credit cards/loans.*

Note: The above paragraph is very important to remember and not just for "delinquent child support payments" but also delinquency on debt in general (credit-card bills, loans, mortgages). The author at one point was rejected for joining the Airforce and the Coast Guard, regardless if it was a cook position, and/or a military intelligence position for having an inadequate credit score at the time. The author was also rejected by joining the Los Angeles Police Department for

Female Privileges in America!
Exposing Feminist Hypocrisy!

having insufficient credit. The author also was denied applications for apartments (even when I made more than 3x the amount in rent) for having insufficient credit. The author was also denied access to loans, credit cards, and student loans due to insufficient credit. The author was also denied dishwasher jobs at fancy restaurants (hotels) for not having sufficient credit. Now the author currently has good credit. But the point is, having a bad credit score (and stupid older-generation-ivy-league-school-silver-spoon-fed-politiciaans don't understand this) in the 21st century, in the United States can bring many financial burdens on you, and it can destroy all of your hopes and dreams that you thought that this country could some day offer and deliver to you but every day refuses to deliver on all of your hopes and dreams that have always been expected for years. That's why I'm warning everyone to build your credit and stabilize it always, because if you don't, you will be a slave to debt and a slave to the credit bureaus who could give two shits about you except their profits.

- *Garnishing of your tax refunds (Maybe Uncle Sam won't touch your state/federal tax return, but the courts will), workers compensation payments, (that you're supposed to receive because you were injured while working for your employer in order to earn money), and disability payments (you probably shouldn't be having kids if you're disabled anyway but if you did have some children prior to being disabled, and you rely on your disability payments to get by, but the courts don't give a*

Female Privileges in America!
Exposing Feminist Hypocrisy!

shit); will occur to you men out there. ***This sexist abuse generally only happens to men and not to women who owe child support to men because "the courts would never want to take credibility or responsibility for depriving women of economical and beneficial opportunities since the courts observe women as the inferior and weaker sex/gender and yet will never publicly admit this."***

- *If you owe more than $2,500 in child support payments, and you own a passport, you can forget about traveling anywhere outside of the United States since your passport will more than likely be revoked over time. The author agrees and understands this deprivation only because there could be a chance (this also includes dead-beat moms) that a parent may start a new life in a different country and never give two-shits about his or her offspring and therefore is held unaccountable for paying child support.*
- *Last (and it probably really isn't the last) but certainly not the least, is jail time. That's right! If the courts see persistent failure for the single father to pay child support, the judge will not hesitate (usually and initially it's through warnings first; after multiple court hearings/proceeding) to put you in jail for however long the judge feels that you should be in jail for. The jail-sentencing-time varies upon which city, county, and state that you reside in. But the point is, even your freedom can be taken away from you for failing to pay child support. The author can agree that men should go*

Female Privileges in America!
Exposing Feminist Hypocrisy!

to jail for consistent failure to pay child support to their offspring on the condition that he is required to find work in jail and all of his payments will be garnished and given towards his child; but only in these circumstances. Other than that, there is no benefit or point on behalf of the child for the alleged dead-beat dad to remain in jail because it only increases the fathers chances and opportunities of being incapable of making faster and greater financial payments towards his offspring.

Isn't it expected that this chart only biasedly shows the percentages of fathers who owe child support payments and not mothers who owe child support payments to fathers? This chart was retrieved from the website www.contemporaryfamilies.org and published in 2018.

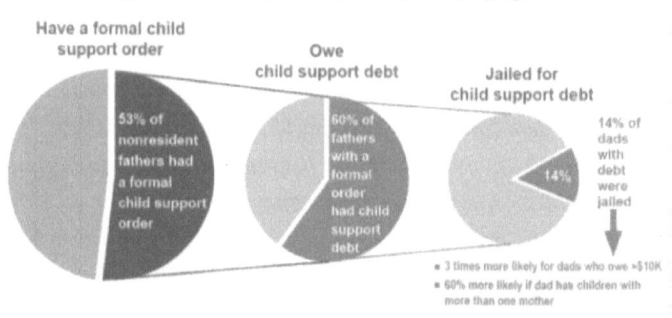

Note: I'm assuming at this point, the percentage rate for fathers owing child support has increased and will continue to

Female Privileges in America!
Exposing Feminist Hypocrisy!

increase, since separations and divorces are very common in the United States today; and especially after these couples have children together. Isn't it ironic how responsible these women were to breed with alleged irresponsible men and then ask the courts to force these men to give her money for their child or children in at least 53% of confirmed cases? At least, according to this chart on the "left circle." 53% of non-resident fathers had a formal child support order. In the middle circle, it reveals 60% of these fathers that had a formal order had child support debt. It could be due to negligence on their behalf or because of unforeseen circumstances (a fucked up economy) like women experience when they get pregnant and refuse to get an abortion when the man does not want children and has even reminded her of this prior to getting her pregnant. In the end, she makes the final decision because "it's her body, and her choice." But because she made the choice to have the child, and even if you only had sex once together which is more than enough to get her pregnant, she will make you financially accountable for child support payments for 18 years (if not more) and the courts will gleefully enjoy doing this for her to ensure that she is rewarded for her mistakes and failures to evaluate a responsible and ethical man. In the right circle, we have 14% of dads that were delinquent in child support payments and as a result, these alleged dead-beat dads were inevitably sent to jail. 14% sounds very little when compared to 100%. However, 14% of 60% of fathers who are delinquent in child support payments (in 2018) today was nearly a 1/4th margin of a guaranteed opportunity for fathers in that year to be incarcerated for failing to pay either little or

Female Privileges in America!
Exposing Feminist Hypocrisy!

nothing of child support payments. In other words, if a quarter population of fathers who owed child support debt impose a risk on themselves to be incarcerated by failing to make child support payments, than the numbers are probably higher today because of the current Covid-19 pandemic, which has deprived millions of single fathers economically; and pretty much destroyed the economy (let's face it). Yet, if only 15% of women owe child support to men in all of child support cases (at the current moment), and have to pay less money to the custodial father, than obviously a woman probably has a greater chance of being struck by lighting at her own wedding than she is to be incarcerated for failing to pay child support to the custodial father.

Note: The author attempted to seek and search any information relating to women being incarcerated for failure to pay child support in regards to a "specific percentage" and was unable to do so because there's not enough women or any women at all being incarcerated enough to make official articles, headlines, or for professional analysts who work for the state/federal government to do so to properly document these cases. Instead, the priority is focused exclusively on men. Here is another chart which confirms and proves that irresponsible women who got pregnant, and decided to have her child are conveniently given advantages and benefits regardless if she is the custodial parent or not, and/or if she is making child support payments to the custodial father. If this isn't obvious sexism and biasness behavior inflicted upon men

Female Privileges in America!
Exposing Feminist Hypocrisy!

by courts, in favor of women, then the words "sexism" and "biases" are either cherry-picked or they don't exist.

Mitchell & Crunk ATTORNEYS AT LAW   DIVORCE   ADOPTIONS   CHILD CUSTODY   PRICES AND COSTS ⌄   TH

Note: This article is both true and false based on my own personal experiences. No, the author has never owed child support before to any blood-money-sucking woman because he does not have kids and refuses to have any in his lifetime! I get to keep all of my benefits!
Here's what's false about this article/statement from an accredited attorney's website.

1. *If men are the primary custodial parent and the mother only receives the child even 40% or 30% or maybe even as low as 20% percent during the week, men will more than likely refrain from taking the mother to court just to get child support payments because men generally are*

Female Privileges in America!
Exposing Feminist Hypocrisy!

proud enough to take care of things on their own; regardless of financial burdens and obstacles. Men tend to also be more understanding and less vindictive than women and therefore, do not demand child support payments (regardless if the woman is or isn't financially stable) as a punishment like common American women practice today in the 21st century.

2. *It's also fair to assume (and I'm positive this happens on a consistent basis) that courts (as it is they never really do) are not always going to demand a woman to pay child support even if she is not the custodial parent regardless if she spends 50% of the time with the child during the week or less than 50% of the time. But if the tables were turned, and the father only spends 40% and even perhaps 50% of the time with the child and/or children, then he more than likely would be required to pay child support. In other words, women get off easy from the same required responsibilities that both parents have to commit to which is towards their offspring.*

Note: These were the only two inaccuracies that I observed in this published web-page. Here are the following accuracies that I can confirm from this published web-page.

1. It is true that more women are becoming more successful in the workforce, (which contradicts the feminist accusation that there is only male privilege in the United States). Although, there is still a pay-gap and there always will be a pay-gap between men and

Female Privileges in America!
Exposing Feminist Hypocrisy!

women, because men by nature, do more dangerous jobs than women, work longer hours than women, and are less likely to request time off due to pregnancy and/or other non-serious emergencies as women; which women often request on their own initiative. Nobody puts a gun to their head for women to refuse to work dangerous jobs, refuse to work longer hours, and refuse to take time off work because they choose to get and remain pregnant and give birth; in addition to other non-emergency circumstances not related to pregnancies.

2. *It's true that more women are paying more child support today than ever before in American history. However, it's nowhere near as close as a higher- margin compared to men who are ordered to pay child support payments towards their offspring. This published web-page desires or at least attempts to "establish equality" between men and women who are ordered to pay child support, therefore attempting to remind the reader that more women are probably suffering more today because they're ordered to pay child support while earning a lesser wage. However, with the exception of rare circumstances, nothing prevents women from earning more money than men or using birth control methods to prevent pregnancies.*

3. *It's also true that more men today are being selected to be the primary custodial parent either on their own initiative & request, or because of a victory-ruling from the court for them. There's too many reasons,*

Female Privileges in America!
Exposing Feminist Hypocrisy!

speculations, and theories for this new embracing opportunity for men to be the primary custodial parent; which is why I find it very difficult to believe that the majority of fathers who refuse to pay child support towards his own offspring is because of his lack of empathy towards his offspring rather than vindictiveness and spitefulness from the opportunistic mother who runs to her nearest court to retrieve money from the father of her child and/or children. Here are some of the reasons why men may be selected to be the primary custodial parents.

- *American Women are working more to provide a more economical environment for their child/children because as of the year, 2022, inflation and the cost of living deprives only one parent of adequately supporting a child, yet alone a household of other occupants who are not children.*
- *American Women are cooking less today in households or refusing to learn to cook as women did in the 1950's because she sees this practice in modern society as an 'inferior duty" to her conscience. Women often use the typical argument of working and being too tired to cook, but plenty of women did this since the founding of our nation and still never complained as much as modern American women do today.*

Female Privileges in America!
Exposing Feminist Hypocrisy!

- American women are less hygienic and clean less today than women in the 1950's, because they see cleaning as an "inferior duty" to their conscience. Women often use the typical argument of working as an excuse not to clean her household; however again, since the founding of our nation, women worked and did clean and hardly ever complained about doing it when compared to modern American women today.
- American women tend to be more mentally and physically abusive towards their children and husbands than ever before in American history; and as a result, the judges see this and probably with reluctance, (it's fair to assume that judges were hesitant to take away a child from the mother regardless if she was a bitch) they end up granting child custody to the father because the father seems more stable, responsible, and logical. **Note: Child neglect is a form of child abuse. Neglect can include refusing to cook, clean, aid, teach, and protect your child. Since women cook, clean, aid, teach and protect their children less today than they ever did before in American history; regardless, if she is a workaholic or lazy mother, these are the results of a woman losing her child/children**.
- Since when do women ever use their cell phone? They never use it! Am I right? Wrong! Almost never, will you ever see a woman not using her

Female Privileges in America!
Exposing Feminist Hypocrisy!

phone. Since women are egotistical and attention-craving creatures, who wants the whole world to know what they're eating, doing, and/or probably fucking, you better beileve that this is one of those qualifications of "neglect for her children" if she spends more time on the phone than nurturing and/or paying attenting to her child/children. It's amazing how women have so much time to surf the internet on the phone and message people and yet she will more than likely never dedicate the same time or even half the time that she spends on her phone towards her child/children or even spend all that wasted time on the cell phone to cook something in the kitchen. **Prove the author wrong about this!**

- *The father was lucky on his official day in court, and that's why he was awarded child custody for his child/children. (This scenario is probably the least logical reason or excuse but hey maybe it has happened in the past but very rarely).*
- *The mother is deceased.*
- *The mother doesn't want the kids (This is more common today than ever before in history but not common enough for fathers to win child custody automatically because of this reason.*
- *The mother has a severe mental and/or physical impairment (if she does she shouldn't be having kids but it's too late to reverse these changes) which deprives her of the opportunity to provide a*

Female Privileges in America!
Exposing Feminist Hypocrisy!

      stable and reasonable financial setting and/or normal environment for her children.
- *The children don't want to live with the mother. Believe it or not, this is a common argument. I, myself, advocated and selected living with my father more than my mother because my mother was a lazy, abusive alcoholic who always got away with her behavior no matter how many times the police came to question her abuse, she was always believed. So, I believe that this reason is more common today than most people would think or question and not because of my personal circumstances but because of other people I've met, heard about, and read about.*

4. It's also true in this web-page article, that many non-custodial mothers aren't even paying child support; when compared to non-custodial fathers. This is either because the man isn't being vindictive, spiteful and demanding payment from the mother or because the mother was able to convince the judge that she should be exempt from making payments because of her personal financial obligations and circumstances. The third option could be that the parents did make an arrangement upon each other for the mother never having to pay child support in order for her to avoid the unnecessary financial burden, embarrassment and time wasting circumstances of filing paperwork at the child support services office (thus benefiting the mother

Female Privileges in America!
Exposing Feminist Hypocrisy!

economically more than the father and the child/children yet again).

5. *It's also true that even though 25% of custodial mothers have not been given child support payments from fathers who are mandated to do so by the courts, that it should also be noted that 32% of custodial fathers are not receiving child support payments from mothers who are mandated to do so by the courts. If a mother has one less mouth to primarily feed (since havings kids today is more expensive when compared to previous decades) since she is the non-custodial parent, assuming she doesn't have any other kids with different fathers, why is it that she either refuses to pay the custodial father or cannot pay? Regardless if women make less than money than men, non-custodial mothers should obtain two jobs if necessary to fulfill her obligations of paying child support to the custodial father; however, being realistic here, since the courts give women an exclusive opportunity to avoid jail time for non-payment of child support, women can abuse this practice and get away with it; and the courts and politicians will do nothing about it because they're sexist cowards and biased towards men.*

Note: Can you imagine how the media and feminist groups would react if women were paying more money in child support payments to men than men pay to women, and if 85% of single fathers receive child support payments while only 15% of single mothers receive child support paymens?

Female Privileges in America!
Exposing Feminist Hypocrisy!

Feminist rallies and liberal women would consistently bitch (they already do about useless arguements), complain, wine, harass their elected-opportunistic-politicians and demand radical changes favoring and benefitting women rather than laws that benefit both men and women equally. So, why don't men complain about this if this is true? It's the same reason why I mentioned earlier in this chapter that women are quick to complain and demand "special treatment" rather than equal treatment. If she receives "equal treatment" from the city, state, and/or federal governments, it's inferior treatment and not good enough! American women generally expect automatic circumstances, events, and/or opportunities for them to be available always and reserved for them exclusively and always in their favor regardless if she's qualified or even earned such special circumstances, events, and/or opportunities. If a woman loses her children to the father in court, the judge is either ignorant or sexist and it's not her fault in any way. Women never accept responsibility at all for things that they do wrong or immoral or anything purely unethical. The only time you will ever hear a woman apologize to a man for her mistakes, errors, and judgements is to her male boss (if she has one) for opportunistic reasons either to kiss ass to get a bigger salary or better promotion. She rarely means her apology though. She still thinks that she was right and that she will always be right; hence that's why she's so quick to run to court and demand child custody and child support payments because she thinks that "she's in the right to receive such exclusive benefits" just by being the first one to ask the judge for these yearly guaranteed benefits which

Female Privileges in America!
Exposing Feminist Hypocrisy!

benefits her economically until her child/children reach the proper adult age. American mothers can be evil in many ways too also by deliberately educating her child/children the following accusations; regardless if it's true or not (which my own mother tried doing to me as I grew older attempting to brainwash me with lies about my father but it never worked); but I'm sure this applies to millions of spiteful vindictive women who are fixated and determined to be so cowardly as to use their own children as a weapon against the child/children's own biological father even if he is an adequate father who at least tries or makes a positive effort for his child/children.

- *Your dad doesn't care about you if he did, he would spend more time with you! Note: Some responsible fathers work too hard (with longer hours) and are unable to sacrifice work-time to see their child/children because men also have to pay their rent/mortgage/bills and does not have the opportunity like women do to marry a new wife and have her pay off all his bills and expenses like the mother has the opportunity of having with a new husband; since women can either work or get married to survive; while men only have the option of working to survive).*
- *Your dad cheated on me and left me for another girl, if he doesn't care about your mother, why would he care about you? He prefers spending his time with other women. Note: While this may apply to some fathers, some women deliberately use this reason whether it's true or not to convince the child/children to begin to*

Female Privileges in America!
Exposing Feminist Hypocrisy!

accept an allegation that women are the priority in the father's life and not his own offspring. First of all, generally a love for your children is different from the same love that you have for your parents and for your partner/spouse. Some of these "love feelings" are stronger for certain relatives, friends, lovers, children, animals, and even objects. Therefore, it's highly unusual that a woman will love her husband (even if it's a happy marriage) more than her children, the same applies to the husband who loves his children more than his wife. This doesn't always happen, but I generally use this as an example because parents often put their children first as "the highest priority" and generally shield them from any mental and/or physical danger rather than themselves. This would indicate and confirm a higher degree for the love of the children by the parents.

- *If you love your mother, you would not go see your father because he doesn't treat your mother well. Note: Women use this "guilt trick" on the child as an effort to convince the child/children that the father is the least priority, and not as great as the mother. It also implies that the father is ruthless and inconsiderate; and if he's this way with the mother, he can be the same way with his children. This could be true; but the point is, American mothers without any reasoning or evidence behind this accusation and also because they're spiteful, and desire to manipulate their own child/children in an effort to make the child/children hate their own father over time, that some of these children end up believing*

Female Privileges in America!
Exposing Feminist Hypocrisy!

their mother and hating their father and it's sad; because in many cases it's not true but the mental damage is already done.

I think it's very important for children to always ask their father his side of the story, rather than always believing the mother, because the mother can be narcissistic and have no problem lying to her children even though she may be a good mother. Let me give you an example, a woman who gets pregnant at 18 years old, and ends up getting pregnant accidentally (which is the primary reason for most pregnancies in the United States), by the time she is 36 years old, and her child is 18 years old, her son or daughter may ask her a very common question that many children ask their parents. "Was I planned?" Most mothers will ultimately reply to their child unequivocally with the four-word response, "yes, honey of course!" Most 18 year old women never and I repeat never plan on getting pregnant. The 18 year-old women that do are ultimately stupid and older logical-thinking people understand this. However, rather than a mother to break her child's heart and admit that he or she was a mistake (which he or she probably was) by saying to her child bluntly, "no, you were not planned" could potentially hurt her child and she does not want that which I understand; but still the mother should be honest even if the truth hurts; after all some people ask themselves periodically to themselves, "why the fuck am I on this planet? What's my purpose here?I know because I'm one of them. I decided to bring this topic up in this chapter "Child Support and Custody" rather than further chapters because in many cases especially during child support custody hearings,

Female Privileges in America!
Exposing Feminist Hypocrisy!

many children are allowed to speak to the judge and render their own personal feelings that they may have towards their parents; and these "personal expressions" by the children can be enough testimony and/or evidence to make the judge render a decision on who is going to be the primary custodial parent and also who is going to end up paying child support. If the mother brainwashes her child to tell the judge "how much of a horrible father he or she has and that the father does not care to live with them" then this only adds more potential victory points for the mother and a lot of economic deprivation and embarrassment for the father in front of the judge and his own family/supporters. There could be no greater revenge-tactic by the mother than to humiliate the father in these methods and circumstances. So, I urge fathers to get more involved with your children, be a better parent to your children than the mother of your child, record and document everything that you do with and for your child that makes you look good and outstanding. Also, the best advice I can give to men is to frequently (I can't stress this enough) ask your children "if the mother bad mouths you and if so, what does she say about you?" This will be your only moment to throw in your side of the story and your personal testimony; so the child can grow up and make his or her own judgements. For now, let's move on to chapter 4 to prove more female privilege in America, if this chapter has not convinced you (the reader) yet of all the benefits and opportunities that women receive and get away with compared to men for the same opportunities/benefits.

Female Privileges in America!
Exposing Feminist Hypocrisy!

IV

-Women are going to colleges more often than men today and still earn less money than men

Female Privileges in America!
Exposing Feminist Hypocrisy!

because it's the woman's fault for choosing a degree that pays less money-

How many times have we heard that women go to colleges and universities more than men? A lot of times! Yet, men are told (as lies) that women do not receive the same benefits as men! How can this false accusation be true if women are going to college and obtaining more knowledge and information about various educational-subjects than men? There's multiple simple reasons for this:

- *The media is operated, approved, and controlled in many cases by women and as a result, these same women desire to distribute false information (fake news to promote feminist ideologies) to establish a false agenda/argument which only benefits them economically. After all, how many young and older women listen to the news and accept the false notion that the entire United States is prejudiced against them which is the primary reason that women make less money than men? Only, ignorant and stupid women follow politicians/celebrities and the media regarding women being given inferior opportunities and benefits than men. The ignorant women believe this because they believe that (possibly, yet subconsciously) anyone who works in politics, entertainment, and/or the media will always be telling the truth and could never lie, or because those same people have suffered in the same*

Female Privileges in America!
Exposing Feminist Hypocrisy!

circumstances and therefore understands these women. However, this is all bullshit!

- *Women have three opportunities to pay for their tuition of their choice, and those choices are to either marry an idiot (generally a man) to pay all of her tuition, or have her parents co-sign for her on student loans, or pay all of the tuition herself (which the woman can't GENERALLY do because she gets paid less; for LESS DANGEROUS WORK AS MEN CONTRIBUTE TO). Men only get two of these options since women will almost never pay for a man's education (unless his mother will pay for her own son's college tuition), yet alone co-sign for student loans for her son which will help pay for these expenses for men who desire to be educated and desire to introduce themselves in the workforce and is willing to do all of the dirty work that women will almost always deny and reject. You read that right! Men have inferior opportunities to go to college than women because women have the advantage, depending on their year of age (generally between 17-32 years of age) because as women age, men will refuse to pay for women's expenses because women become less attractive, more obese, unattractive and unreliable in all economical circumstances (unless they're the baby-boomer generation which had the whole world given to them for nothing and not because they earned such economical advantages but because these women were lucky to be born during economical prosperity times).*

Female Privileges in America!
Exposing Feminist Hypocrisy!

You read these examples and probably wonder why stupid-ass women in the United States probably complain about inequality when women in the United States are given everything to them with or without request. This chapter is dedicated to a confirmation of special treatment that is given to American women when compared to American men. Now, as proof that American women are more blessed, entitled, and given more advantages than American men, let's take a look at all the facts according to the federal government's statistics and analysis!

While some majors are popular for both men and women, some are heavily dominated by one gender or the other.

Below are the top 20 college majors that most women graduate in. Nursing is the heavyweight here, with over 120,000 women graduating with a bachelor's in nursing in 2016. Nursing is also a female-dominated major, with 87% of graduates being women.

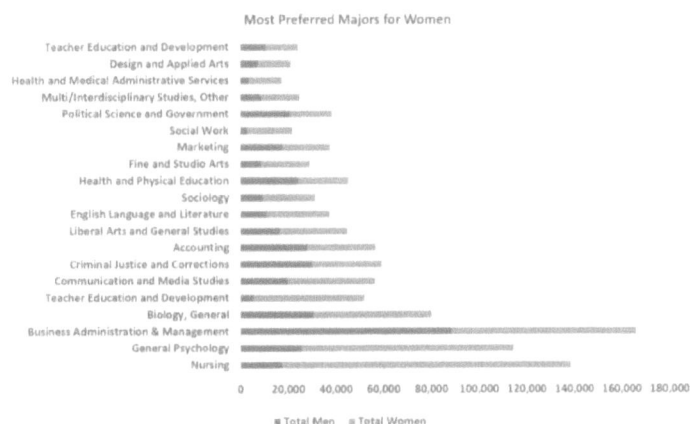

Female Privileges in America!
Exposing Feminist Hypocrisy!

As you can see based on this graph comparing men and women's majors, it clearly shows beyond a reasonable doubt that women intentionally and generally to them (without force) select to be a nurse as their financial career. Nothing stops women from attempting to major in a different field to meet their financial obligations. This graph should prove additional proof beyond a reasonable doubt that men (by choice) select economical degrees that deliver economic prosperity towards them. Now, let's take a look at the average income of female nurses:

- Female nurses in the United States generally earn Depending on his or her state) an average salary amount of $73,500 in the United States of America.

However, we do have false journalists and false representatives who represent the current American media who intentionally mislead the public about facts and only publish their work on opinions and not facts. Here is a fake news publication from a journalist attempting to establish a false argument that women who work the same hours as men (in all states in the United States of America) as a nurse are paid less than men without providing facts. This journalist is a liar and a piece of shit by nature for spreading false information. Let's examine this article and argument by a pansy-guy (Jeff Lagasse) journalist willing to spread fake news just to get a promotion and probably never gets laid (since pro-feminist guys never get laid) even though he probably thinks he will for allegedly

Female Privileges in America!
Exposing Feminist Hypocrisy!

defending women's rights in the work place. Here is the link to this article:

https://www.healthcareitnews.com/news/male-nurses-still-make-6000-plus-more-women-new-survey-shows

Healthcare IT News

In a profession dominated by women, men in nursing earn more than $6,000 more a year than their female counterparts, according to a new survey of more than 4,500 nurses across the country.

The Nursing Salary Research Report, which included registered nurses from all 50 states, showed men earn an average of $79,688 compared to $73,090 for women. Men make up about 12 percent of the U.S. nursing workforce.

"Even taking into account total hours worked, years of nursing experience, age, education level and certification status, men still are making more money than women," said Robert Hess Jr., Nurse.com by OnCourse Learning's executive vice president and chief clinical executive of healthcare, in a statement. "And from our robust research, salary is the most important job factor for nurses across all demographics."

Have you noticed the first sentence already? A "profession that is dominated by women." While this may be true, it's not because women are forced with a gun to their head to become a nurse. Women intentionally and purposely selected "nursing" as their occupation. Therefore, they decided to be paid (before taxes) on average, a salary of $73,090 annually. Have you noticed the second sentence? "The Nursing Salary Research Report included registered nurses from 50 states, showing men earn an average of $79,688 compared to women who earn $73,090." Because of this, there's an average 12% pay-increase for men than women. This may also be true. But here comes the fake part in this half-bullshit article which is

Female Privileges in America!
Exposing Feminist Hypocrisy!

the third paragraph. "Even taking into account total hours worked, years of nursing experience, age, education level and certification status, men still are making more money than women." For the record, this idiot journalist (if he even deserves such credibility to be called that) cites no facts or evidence in his argument. He did attempt to place a link in his article regarding his argument, but after clicking that link, you are redirected to a website to download the Nurse Salary Research Report to read it yourself for answers. Why is this article bullshit? The reason why is because the journalist is creating deception by stating "total hours worked" as one of his arguments on why it's unfair that women are paid less money than men. I have cited multiple reasons and evidence throughout the earlier chapters of this book for the reasons why women earn less money than men, for the same equal hourly-pay or salary that they receive, and in the same position. The primary reason that women get paid less than men is because women will not work the same hours as men. They will not dedicate themselves to do so whether it's because they are lazy or because they have other priorities (children), therefore, women will more than likely request time-off or request to leave early from their shift regardless of what occupation it is. Baby-sitters, relatives, friends, and even day care may not always be reliable. As it is, most women who have children are the primary custodial parents in the United States; so it's fair to at least assume and with common sense, acknowledge that since men are not the primary custodial parents, they have less obligations, and therefore more time to dedicate themselves towards their place of employers,

Female Privileges in America!
Exposing Feminist Hypocrisy!

whenever he so desires. That's not to say that non-custodial fathers are dead-beat dads but since there has already been an established agreement between the mother and father (either through them or the courts) for the mother to be the primary-custodial parent, in which men will generally use and invest their time into making more money. If a male-nurse is ordered or requested to pay child support or does it voluntarily, then you better believe that the single father will more than likely ask and demand more hours in the clinic and/or hospital that he's working in; and this includes other places of employment not in the health industry. This article also mentions "age," "education level," and "certification status," as arguments to his claim, that women are delusional when they claim that they're paid unfairly and therefore the health industry must be deliberately biased against women; even though there's more registered female-nurses in America, then there are registered male-nurses. How biased is that? The only real valuable thing that this journalist mentioned that could substantially be accepted as some credibility (if there is any) is that "men negotiate their salary more often than women prior to being hired." Again, we go back to the point, where women not only decided their own occupation, but they also were unwilling to negotiate a specific salary for their occupation. It's very common for employers during interviews, depending on what the candidate expects regarding a specific hourly-wage or salary, to ask the candidate on how much compensation he or she would like to receive before being hired. If women felt too intimidated to ask for a decent wage or risk being rejected because the interviewer might be biased

Female Privileges in America!
Exposing Feminist Hypocrisy!

against her, that's her fault. True leaders and people who are willing to work hard should never be scared of anything. Now let's move on! Oh, by the way, here's the link that the journalist placed in his webpage. I honestly don't think that he read the whole thing. Neither did I, but I don't have too; because my arguments are more valid and align with logic and common-sense.

https://mediakit.nurse.com/Nursing_Salary_Research_Report?utm_source=press-release&utm_medium=OCL-website&utm_campaign=RNsalary-survey

Now, let's take a look at a different chart where 20 of the major college-degrees which are primarily selected by women in order to use those degrees in an occupation of their choice that is relevant towards their degree! Here is the web-page link that was published in 2017 by Team College Factual using statistics credited to the Department of Education..

https://inside.collegefactual.com/stories/the-most-popular-majors-for-women-men

Female Privileges in America!
Exposing Feminist Hypocrisy!

Below are the top 20 college majors that most women graduate in. Nursing is the heavyweight here, with over 120,000 women graduating with a bachelor's in nursing in 2016 Nursing is also a female-dominated major, with 87% of graduates being women.

According to this comprehensive study, Nursing is the #1 field that women select as their personal careers. It's also a field that employs more women than men. As you can see by this chart, Business Administration and Management and General Psychology come next as popular degrees for women. So on average, how much do these popular degrees that women intentionally select for themselves deliver to them on an annual financial basis on average? Let's take a look at another graph published by the unbiased Department of Education.

Female Privileges in America!
Exposing Feminist Hypocrisy!

Which of the 20 most popular majors for women have the best earning potential? That would be Political Science and Government, which is 46% female-dominated, and where grads earn a median salary of $62,600.

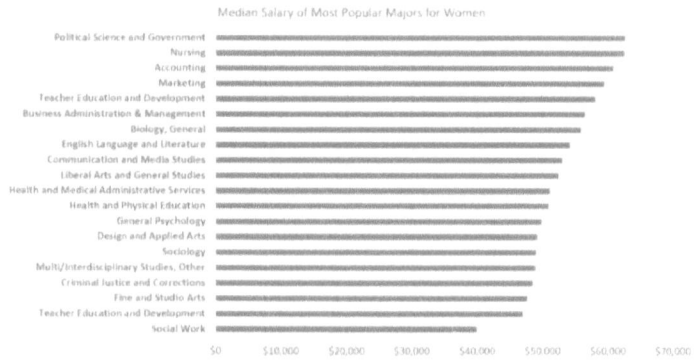

Data sourced from the Department of Education and Payscale.

The average salary for the top 20 most popular majors women choose is $52,800.

The average salary for all of these popular majors (after Political Science & Management) brings an average annual salary between $52,800-$62,000. This is not a lot of revenue to generate but yet again, women decided to major in these fields because of "interest" rather than "logic." Women used their emotions and feelings to major in a degree that they probably think will give them $100,000+ dollars a year but in many cases it's not even half of that. Political Science & Government has been a very popular degree for women since many modern American women today in America have been brainwashed about alleged inequality performances practiced against them by men, corporations, the government; and the entire world. As a result these alleged patriotic women desire to change the

Female Privileges in America!
Exposing Feminist Hypocrisy!

way the government operates (through protests & activism), or become involved in the government themselves (deciding to become a career politician like the majority of opportunistic politicians inevitably become because of all that money, power, fame, respect, fear, and ass-kissing that they receive all of their life as a politician). Modern American women love power and they love controlling and manipulating people (especially men) against their will; which is why the majority of women in Congress are left-wing liberal Democrats. Democrats, since the days of it's foundation supported slavery, and now support mandatory vaccine mandates for Covid-19 despite Covid-19 being a 99% recovery rate without the Covid vaccine. The similarity for slavery and Covid-19 is forcing someone to do something against their own will. A slave prior to the civil war, generally couldn't buy things or own things, or go to Broadway theaters or retail stores on their own to own anything without the expressed approval of the slave owner. Now in certain cities in America, if you refuse to take the covid vaccine which has already killed over 10,000 (probably more than what's being currently admitted) people, then you can't go to movie theaters, gyms, or retail outlets. Doesn't this sound like segregation and slavery, forcing people not to do what they joyfully enjoy doing, which is shopping and/or seeking entertainment. You're probably wondering, what does this have to do with this chapter? What does Covid-19 have to do with women going to college more than men? A lot actually. Since women go to college more than men now at a higher rate, it's women who can help make a positive difference for the majority of Americans since they generally

Female Privileges in America!
Exposing Feminist Hypocrisy!

select a degree that involves politics and policies but are biased and very selective themselves and probably vindictive in their practices as they're in relationships with partners when things go sour. It's not a surprise that women put little to no effort as a career politician themselves once they're in office towards their constituents. Here is a study of a recent polling data that was recorded in August of 2021, but published on a statista's web-page by Erin Duffin on September, 6th, 2021 and the link: https://www.statista.com/statistics/207579/public-approval-rating-of-the-us-congress/

U.S. Congress - public approval rating 2020-2021
Published by Erin Duffin, Sep 6, 2021

The most recent polling data from August 2021 puts the approval rating of the United States Congress at 28 percent. This is slightly higher than the previous month when Congressional approval stood at 26 percent. Over the past 12 months, Congressional approval hit a high in March 2021, at 36 percent approval.

Congressional approval

Congressional approval, particularly over the past few years, has not been high. Americans tend to see Congress as a group of ineffectual politicians who are out of touch with their constituents. Despite the current Congress having the largest number of women and being the most diverse Congress in American history, very little has been done to improve the opinion of Americans regarding the legislative branch.

Ye of little faith

However, Americans tend not to have much confidence in institutions in the United States. While confidence in the military and small business is quite high, everything from the police to the medical system to organized labor are much more controversial. But even in this case, confidence in Congress continues to inspire very little confidence in the American public.

According to this recent polling and published graph-chart, Congress has a 28% approval rating.

Female Privileges in America!
Exposing Feminist Hypocrisy!

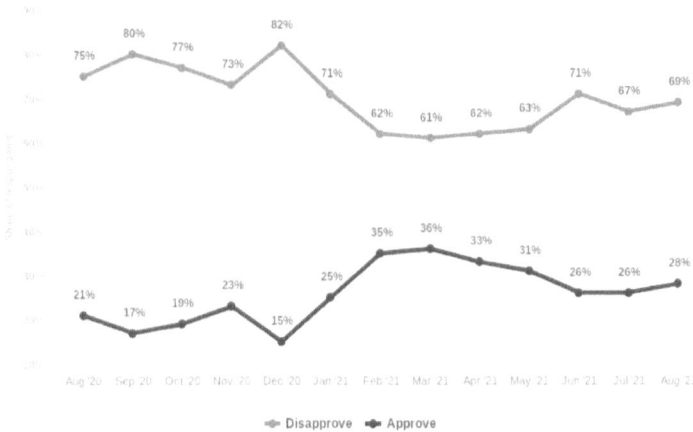

This is barely just over 1/4th or a quarter of our members of Congress. It's really pathetic. Now, this article mentions that "despite the current Congress having the largest number of women and being the most diverse Congress in American history, very little has been done to improve the opinion of Americans regarding the legislative branch." While I do understand that men are the primary members of Congress, this still does not explain why Congress has a current low rating. That's just Congress! Imagine state and city governments where many of the politicians in the states are women and do nothing worth-remembering during their tenure in office. So, what's the point, you might ask? The point is since women may not want to use their brain in politics (they often never do), they could serve a purpose by majoring in a different degree that pays them more money on the condition that they build things with their hands (computers, bridges,

Female Privileges in America!
Exposing Feminist Hypocrisy!

buildings, new technology etc). Now let's take a look at the majority of majors that men select as a career. Remember! Men don't always necessarily pick a degree because they "think it's pretty" but because that degree offer them more money and also more opportunities since there will be less competition for those jobs in the job market, since people don't generally want those jobs; especially women who want a convenient atmosphere that offers the least amount of physical-labor as possible. Again, this graph-chart is from the Department of Education stating 20 of the most popular degrees that men generally select for their occupations relevant to their degree. You will first notice the jobs that require dedication, physical labor (getting your hands dirty) creating, and researching that men are willing to do which may sound boring and not entertaining to some people, but it's still necessary for our nations technological advances and national security and it comes with generous compensation but with excessive responsibilities. Men are more capable by nature to handle excessive responsibilities while women become overburdened and are quick to complain or run and hide when faced with regular work responsibilities other than motherhood. Believe me, I've seen this all of my life in the working field and with women politics; citing Vice President Kamala Harris as a perfect example.

Female Privileges in America!
Exposing Feminist Hypocrisy!

The Most Popular Degrees For Men

The following chart represents the 20 majors with the largest amounts of men in them (it doesn't necessarily mean the major is male-dominated as more women go to college than men).

As you can see there is some overlap in the lists. Nursing, business administration, biology and psychology are popular with men as well as women.

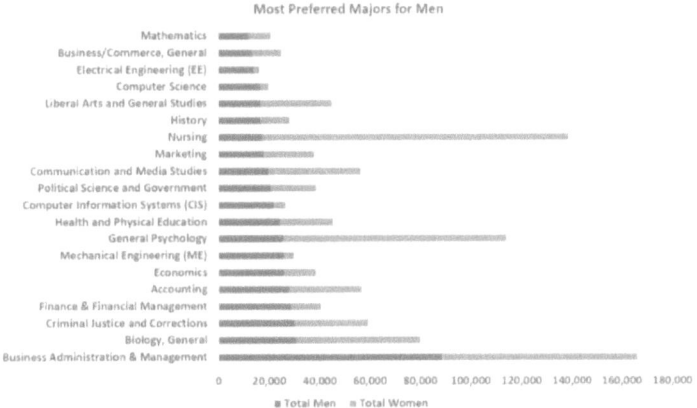

Poor poindexter! I bet in the beginning in high school and college, women often ignored and rejected him because of his excessive studying in the related job-fields above the graph-chart in which includes these studies:

- Mathematics
- Electrical Engineering
- Computer Science (Go, poindexter, go!)
- Mechanical Engineering
- Computer Information System (CIS)
- Finance & Financial Management
- Economics
- History

Female Privileges in America!
Exposing Feminist Hypocrisy!

- Business Administration & Management

Now let's take a look at the graph-chart (again from the Department of Education) that highlights men's financial success that they achieve more than women "because of all of these majors that men personally selected because of the future benefits and success that these degrees may offer with less competition in the job market."

Data from the Department of Education

Despite the overlap, the average salaries of the most popular for men is higher, mainly due t the presence of more science and math heavy majors appearing on the list.

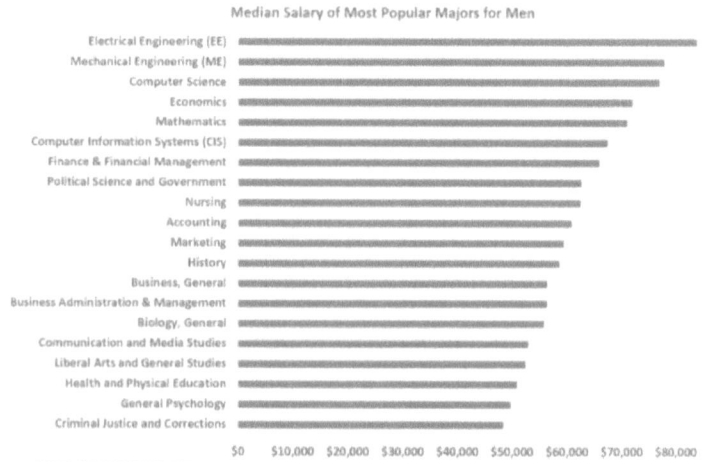

Did you read the first sentence in this graph-chart? "Men's salaries tend to be higher than women because of their decision to major in science and math related-degrees." This is no longer an already opinionated example from the author of this book, but a confirmation from the Department of Education.

Female Privileges in America!
Exposing Feminist Hypocrisy!

Why would they lie, and what benefit do they have to make these charts up? When Poindexter majored in math and science in college, and was doing so well in these subjects in high school, he probably was overlooked, and unpopular. But, the degree paid off for him a decade or two later, where poindexter makes a lot of money and can have young cheerleaders now if he wants that he could not get when he was in high school and college because poindexter had nothing attractive on his plate so he choose to study rather than to get laid like some jocks and rebels. Good for you poindexter! Many men are willing to make these kinds of sacrifices for themselves in order to expedite and establish their own personal prosperity agenda for their future. Women don't generally make sacrifices for themselves. Women expect others to make sacrifices for them in order for them to financially succeed and it first begins in high school when men have to offer to pay and take them to the prom because women feel entitled to receive but not to give. It takes time and effort to study, learn, and practice science and mathematical equations, and formulas, and by studying these unpopular subjects, men have the advantage of discovering and/or inventing a product, artificial intelligence, and/or discovering lost technology and putting it's practice into use. A lot more benefits can arise from this especially for the reputation of the United States. Scientists and engineers interest men because men desire to learn something new whether it's interesting, controversial, and/or unpopular. As a result of this, men will always be credited with making discoveries and inventing new technology. That's not to say that a woman with a business degree can't invent a website or

Female Privileges in America!
Exposing Feminist Hypocrisy!

an app for her business or a woman who majors in a nursing degree doesn't understand medicine. It only means that the female-nurse may understand certain medications and how to practice medicine to patients, but does not understand or know the ingredients and/or recipes that make up medications and vaccines; and in this case, generally scientists (of many fields) and virologists understand the ingredients and recipes that are necessary to make the medications and vaccines. Nurses don't know this information, they only know what the doctor tells them and what kind of medication/vaccine to provide to the patient. Hence, the more knowledge and information that you know in science and math, the more potential economic opportunities you may embrace. You don't need to be a genius to be a registered nurse or have a business degree. Therefore, those degrees that are Business & Management and Nursing will not give a generous salary unless of course you use the business degree's knowledge to open up a business and the nursing degree to likewise open up a clinic or billing-coder business or if you end up working for the city, state or federal government which many Americans with these degrees are not employed by the city, state or federal government. The truth hurts, but it's the truth. At the end of the study of the degrees that men and women pursue is a comprehensive additional article that was published by researchers at Cornell University.

Female Privileges in America!
Exposing Feminist Hypocrisy!

Do women choose lower-paying majors, or is there descrimination against women no matter their choice?

Researchers from Cornell University determined that it is the choice of career that largely determines the differences in pay between men and women. In other words, women dominate jobs that pay less, like early childhood education or social work, while men dominate jobs that tend to pay more.

But is it as simple as getting more women to choose an engineering major over sociology?

Maybe not. Other studies seem to indicate that when more women move into a job field, the pay across the field goes down. Women nurses, doctors, and lawyers, for example, all get paid less than their male counterparts.

Apparently, the trend works both ways. For example, the field of computer programming historically was lower paying when it was dominated by women, and as more men became interested the pay and prestige has increased.

It's always going to be difficult to determine how much of a pay gap is due to gender bias and how much of it is due to difficult-to-measure factors. Do the women in those fields get penalized for taking time off to parent? Do the men in those fields choose niche specializations that pay more, or are they more aggressive in asking for more pay?

How much is a women's choice in a college major and career impacted by the bias she has encountered in her own life, and how much of it is due to natural preferences?

The good news is that despite the difficulties, the gender pay gap has been decreasing steadily. As more women go to college and become educated about what fields will provide the best options hopefully it will continue to decrease.

It confirms beyond any doubt all of my arguments that I've included in this chapter but "which is that women earn less than men because of their decision to major in a field that does not compensate them as much as other degrees such as mechanical engineering, science, and computers." The first paragraph makes sense in this article, and in a different section of the article, where it states a question, if "women are penalized for taking time off to be a parent?" Of, course they have every right to be penalized if she misses work or not regardless of the reason. Businesses are not supposed to work around a person's schedule, an employee is supposed to work around a businesses schedule. Just because a woman has a

Female Privileges in America!
Exposing Feminist Hypocrisy!

child does not give her supreme priority over people who don't have children regarding work schedules. The rest of this article is all pro-feminist bullshit nonsense that attempts to express pity against women who earn less than men because of alleged "biasedness" in the work field that is allegedly practiced against them. Of course, their arguments and theories are not a fact which is why this article asks more questions than it does have answers if you read it. My arguments are facts and are not theories. **Prove me wrong!** I wanted to include this photograph showing the difference between a woman (Laura) borrowing money from banks, to pay off her student loans which averages $30,000-$150,000 debt, and still cannot get a job with her degree, yet assumes people who are not college educated are idiots (and probably won't even date a man who does not have a college degree), when compared to a man (Brian) who worked in a 4-5 year apprentice, is nearly debt-free, makes $80,000-$150,000 a year in compensation, and because Laura didn't pay her electricity, Brian is trained and skilled to cut off her electricity.

Female Privileges in America!
Exposing Feminist Hypocrisy!

LAURA
- 4 year degree for a job in a saturate market
- $150k in debt
- no job
- thinks people who don't go to 4 year college are stupid

BRIAN
Went to work in a 4 - 5 year apprentice
- Debt free...
- Makes 80k - 150k a year.
- Cuts Laura's power for non payment.

The truth is that it would be wrong for anyone to feel pity and sorry for this woman who couldn't get a job for these three reasons alone:

- You know the economy is changing rapidly and so is the job market because of upgraded technology and politics, so you should have done your homework and research to see which degrees will be in high-demand in the

Female Privileges in America!
Exposing Feminist Hypocrisy!

future rather than what degree that you expressed interest in because it's fun, popular, and meets your convenient lifestyle to brag to all your friends and relatives about.
- You choose this degree. Nobody forced you to major in this degree, fill out an application to enroll in a college, much less sign on the dotted line to get financial aid and student loans for your degree. You did all of this; therefore, whether you benefit or lose as result of these actions, this will entirely be your fault.
- You could have found a job with your useless degree, but turned down many job offers because of your ego which you think that "you're too superior" to be working in an environment and/or atmosphere like that, and since it either doesn't pay the salary that you desire, or because you're embarrassed that you spent so much money on a useless degree, you don't want your friends and relatives to know where you work and what you do, or you're just plain lazy and feel entitled to receive government welfare and benefits as your method of financial support. There is no fourth option in this matter, so you would have to pick one of these reasons.

Brian didn't care what people thought about what he did or wanted to do with his life, and he did not care about doing dangerous jobs like climbing up an electric pole to turn on or off someone's electricity like Laura's. This doesn't make him a bad guy for depriving people of electricity anymore than an executioner kills a convicted killer on death row. This is their duties and jobs. No one said it was intended to be fun, like

Female Privileges in America!
Exposing Feminist Hypocrisy!

being a movie star actor, or Vice President of a fortune 500 corporation because of all that wealth that you receive and all that ass kissing that you get from opportunists. What's even more sad and pathetic (I don't agree with this law but again this is her fault) that if Laura doesn't pay back her student loans, because she refuses to work for whatever reasons, then her credit will be destroyed and if she files for Chapter 7 (bankruptcy) or Chapter 13 (bankruptcy), legally she is still liable to pay every penny back to the banks. There's no escaping this, except death of course. I also want to point out before I end this chapter that I do not believe all degrees are useless; but I do believe that only a handful of degrees in the United States are worth getting and valuable economically towards your personal interest in many ways; even if the job that you get from your degree is so damn boring that you can't wait to go home once your shift ends, and don't look forward to going back to work the next day. *For now, let's move on to chapter 5 to prove more female privilege in America, if this chapter has not convinced you (the reader) yet of all the benefits and opportunities that women receive and get away with compared to men for the same opportunities/benefits then hopefully the next chapter will; for the truth shall establish pure reality on current practices and benefits that American women practice and receive; and also a reminder that men will never receive these same benefits as American women unless the man works his ass off for the rest of his life.*

Female Privileges in America!
Exposing Feminist Hypocrisy!

-Women receive more benefits and special treatment than men in the military-

I know exactly what you're thinking! How the hell is this even possible? After all, women can now select a combat position as an infantry soldier in the United States Army, like men have been doing since December 13th, 1636 (the foundation of the Army National Guard). Just because a woman can select a combat position in the military does not mean that she receives equal treatment from her commanding officers. Let me first start off with procedures that are required from recruits at their selected basic training locations. These requirements are not the same for men and women. Here are some examples:

- *Women are not required to shave their heads as men have to in all military branches (Marines, Army, Navy, Coast Guard, & Air Force & probably the newly-established Space Force).*
- *Men are specifically hand-picked and selected to go to combat more than women, and if men have a different military occupational specialty other than a front-line combat position, the man will have his MOS changed against his will to be forced to be in a front-line combat position rather than a woman in the military being forced to change her MOS. In other words, women are given convenient status to avoid having her life be put at risk through combat because the military wants to give women superior and special treatment more than men.*

Female Privileges in America!
Exposing Feminist Hypocrisy!

- Women's physical fitness tests/examinations/initial strength-tests are reduced (to make it more convenient for them to pass) than men. Note: This is not equal pay for equal work, because an E-1 female recruit in basic training has the same basic pay (does not include other forms of pay or benefits such as bonuses) as a male recruit who is also an E-1, yet the female recruit is required to perform less physical fitness exercises and tests than men have to do in order to graduate from basic training yet alone even enlist in the United States Marine Corps.

Here's proof of that in these examples so you know the author's not bullshitting! I wonder why these modern feminists never complain about this to Congress or the military! After all, why would they? Women can get paid the same as men but perform less work, isn't that what they always desire? This first example is from the official Marines.com website that displays its initial strength test requirements for both men and women that must be fulfilled prior to enlisting (as of 2021).

Female Privileges in America!
Exposing Feminist Hypocrisy!

INITIAL STRENGTH TEST

To even begin recruit training, aspiring Marines must pass the Initial Strength Test (IST). It is recommended that recruits report to training with scores well above the minimum standards. The IST consists of the following tests:

FOR ALL APPLICANTS

PULL UPS / PUSH UPS

Male: 3 pull-ups or 34 push-ups (2:00 time limit)

Female: 1 pull-up or 15 push-ups (2:00 time limit)

Do you see what I see and read what I read? Men are given a 2:00 time limit to perform 3 pull-ups or 34 push-ups, while women are given a 2:00 time limit to do 1 pull-up or 15 push-ups! Does that sound equal? Doesn't this sound sexist and biased towards the man? Were not done yet though! Let's take a look at the required running standards & planks or crunches that men and women marine applicants have to achieve prior to enlisting. It's pretty pathetic too because you would think that Marine Corps would not be biased or sexist towards any gender because that military branch is allegedly supposed to be the most physically demanding and most powerful military branch out of all military branches serving the United States. Apparently, even today (as of 2021) the Marines are biased against their own applicants and sexist towards men!

Female Privileges in America!
Exposing Feminist Hypocrisy!

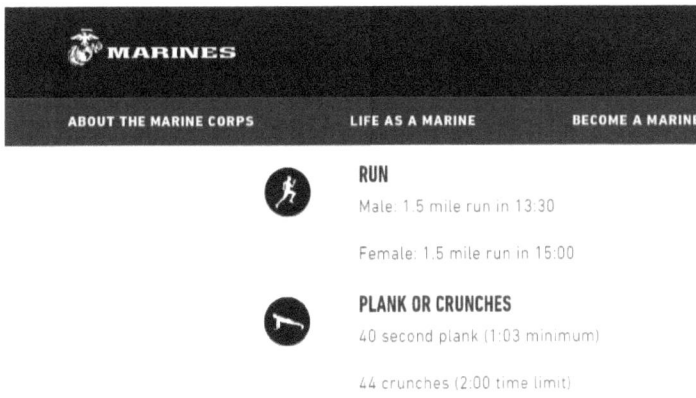

Men get the "distinct honor" of having to run 1.5 miles in 13:30 (a minute and a half less) minutes in order to sign his contract to join the Marines, while women get the "distinct privilege" to run 1.5 miles in 15:00 minutes in order for her to sign the contract to join the marines. What if this mandate and requirements were the other way around? What if women had to run 1.5 miles in 13:30 like men have to, but men have to run 1.5 miles in only 15:00? How many female-feminist-journliasts (who probably never served in the military themselves) will bitch, complain, and claim sexism from the military geared towards them? The answer is a lot! Why? Because, women assume and think that "their patriots" if only they voice their opinions, never mind standing with a weapon in a combat position to defend their country which many feminist women will refuse to do. The only thing that is equal between men and women in this bullshit sexist test is a 40-second plank (with a 1:03 minute time limit) and/or 44 crunches (within a 2:00 minute time limit). But crunches are way easier than running

Female Privileges in America!
Exposing Feminist Hypocrisy!

or doing pull-ups or sit-ups. So, therefore, the Marines decides to make this section of the initial strength test easy for both men and women equally. However, since it's three tests, men have to perform better by 2/3rds with a reduced time limit (the pull-up section and the running section) compared to women. Women only have to perform 1/3rd of physical fitness tests equally good to men while having an increased time limit in order to qualify to serve in the Marines. Why can't these tests be administered equally to both genders for the same maximum time given to each of them? Is the Marine Corps being too nice and lenient towards women and being too harsh and irrational towards men? We all know the answer to these questions! Now, let's move forward to the actual "physical fitness test" that Marines have to pass annually until their discharge from the Marines. You would think that the military was being lenient towards marine-women applicants, and their leniency would end, once they sign their contract, but that's not the case. Women in the Marines still receive special treatment to this very day and it's pathetic and immoral.

Female Privileges in America!
Exposing Feminist Hypocrisy!

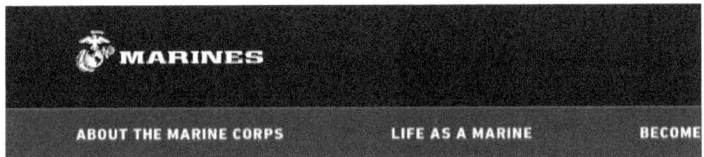

PHYSICAL FITNESS TEST

The Marine Corps Physical Fitness Test, or PFT, evaluates stamina and physical conditioning. It includes 3 parts: pull-ups or push-ups, crunches or plank pose, and a 3-mile timed run. Pull-ups and push-ups are essential to building the upper body strength necessary to win battles. Crunches and planks are critical to maintaining a strong core and being battle-ready at a moment's notice. Males must complete the three-mile run in 28 minutes or less. Females must complete the three-mile run in 31 minutes or less.

There really is no point to mention or even investigate how many pull-ups, push-ups, planks, and crunches are necessary for each gender to perform in order for them to continue to be contracted to the Marines. However, you can still see sexist/biased behavior geared towards men than women in this bullshit test. Men have to complete a three-mile run in 28 minutes or less, while women get to complete this three-mile run in 31 minutes or less. 3 minutes might not sound like a lot, but believe me, when you're running, and you're given a time limit, it makes a difference; especially if you're an amateur runner. It also makes you wonder if many women who are currently Marines today truly earned thier position to be a Marine since they were given lenient physical training requirements to enlist and continue to be enlisted? Now, let's take a look at the standards for men and women in the Army. By the way, the Army is the biggest military branch serving the

Female Privileges in America!
Exposing Feminist Hypocrisy!

United States, but even their branch is just as biased and sexist towards men than towards women.

HAIR & APPEARANCE REQUIREMENTS

Serving in the Army requires a clean and well-groomed appearance, but the freedom you'll have to express your individuality may surprise you. While there are rules in place to ensure your safety and general uniformity among Soldiers, other restrictions have been modified to respect religious and personal expression.

HAIRCUTS & HAIRSTYLES

✓ PERMITTED FOR WOMEN
- Completely shaved or closely-shaved hair (may be tapered in appearance and if hair doesn't part naturally, a straight part may be cut in)
- Short or medium length hair (not extending beyond the lower edge of the collar)
- Medium length hair may be worn in a ponytail if you're unable to form a bun due to hair length or texture (must not interfere with the ability to wear authorized headgear)
- Long hair worn neatly pinned above the lower edge of the collar
- Long hair worn in a ponytail centered on the back of your head during physical training or tactical operations (except when considered a safety hazard)
- Plain hair accessories used to secure your hair that aren't distracting or decorative
- Hair extensions that have the same general appearance as your natural hair
- Hair highlights with natural colors that blend together in a subtle and natural way
- Hair dyes, tints, or bleaches that match your natural hair color
- Wigs that look natural (may not be used to cover unauthorized hairstyles)
- Hair worn in multiple styles, such as braided twists or locs with a side twist to secure hair, as long as style is neat in appearance and doesn't impact proper wear of headgear

✗ NOT PERMITTED FOR WOMEN
- Bulky hairstyles or extremely long hair that interferes with the ability to wear headgear or protective equipment
- Dyes, tints, or bleaches that do not match your natural hair color
- Steel hair picks
- Trendy and exaggerated hairstyles, including shaved portions of the scalp or designs cut into your hair
- Loose hair (while in uniform)
- Extreme or dramatic updo styles (while in uniform)

Here are the standards for Army recruits to have, prior to attending basic training in the Army. Do you notice the first opportunity (not a requirement)? "Completely shaved or closely shaved hair (maybe tampered in appearance and if hair doesn't part naturally, a straight part may be cut in)." How many women who join the military, regardless of the branch, voluntarily raise their hands up to have all of their beautiful hair shaved?

Female Privileges in America!
Exposing Feminist Hypocrisy!

Monday, January 18, 2021
Carson Frame / American Homefront Project

This picture is credited (yet authentic) to https://www.kpbs.org/news/2021/jan/18/covid-19-forces-military-scale-back-basic-training/.
This picture was taken sometime in 2021, but the interesting thing is to look at all of these "allegedly qualified" army recruits who still have their hair-buns in a ponytail and more realistically, be able to keep their hair, unlike Army men recruits. Hypocrisy and sexism are at it's best performance and action in this picture. Look at the drill sergeant observing these recruits as he is clearly photographed without being given the opportunity to have hair for himself. Maybe this was his choice, but regardless of his choice, and even if this drill

Female Privileges in America!
Exposing Feminist Hypocrisy!

sergeant enjoys being bald, these are the requirements for male drill sergeants and not required for female drill sergeants. Female privilege exists in our greatest and largest military branch even in the most basic standards such as haircuts. Yet, when we look at the requirements for men, women can receive 11 regulated haircuts (to their requests) but men can only receive 4 regulated haircuts at their own request. Again, another sexist and biased action towards men and this is men and women working for the federal government so you would think equality is established between both of these genders. These are federal occupations. The answer is no! Fuck men, bless women; that really is the slogan at this point from our federal government.

✓ **PERMITTED FOR MEN**
- Completely shaved or closely-trimmed hair (if hair does not part naturally, you may cut a straight part into the hair or style the hair with one part)
- Sideburns that don't extend below the bottom opening of the ear
- Hair highlights with natural colors that blend together in a subtle and natural way
- Wigs or hairpieces used to cover natural baldness or disfiguration

✗ **NOT PERMITTED FOR MEN**
- Braids, cornrows, twists, or locs (while in uniform or in civilian clothes on duty)
- Shaved designs cut into hair or scalp
- Styled sideburns that taper, flair, or come to a point

FACIAL HAIR
- Men must keep their face clean-shaven (when in uniform, or in civilian clothes on duty)
- Mustaches must be neatly trimmed, tapered, and tidy
- Beards may be worn for religious reasons but must be worn in a neat and conservative manner

RELIGIOUS GARMENTS (HIJABS, TURBANS, KIPPOT)
- Religious headgear may be worn in solid, subdued colors that closely resemble assigned uniforms (generally black, brown, green, tan, or navy blue)
- Soldiers wearing a combat uniform may wear a hijab, turban, or under-turban in a matching camouflage pattern
- Hair worn under the turban is not subject to general standards, but may not fall over the ears or eyebrows or touch the collar while in uniform

Female Privileges in America!
Exposing Feminist Hypocrisy!

The facts remain that American women, generally, are priveleged and receive special treatment from men, policies, and statutes in which these feminist women select to ignore, yet understand, but will always find an excuse to claim that "men are given superior treatment compared to women" which is a bullshit lie and emotional feeling from their behalf. I challenge every feminist and woman living in America to challenge all of my arguements and prove the author of this book wrong! Nothing stops them! Additionally, nothing will stop my responses towards their challenges against me! This book is written to establis the truth; and not ot fictionalized or establish a fantasy world in which generally, American women seek to believe in and accept. This book is accurate and non-fiction; and does belong in every library across America in the non-fiction section of every library; especailly the library of Congress. Let this be a reminder to all women who desire to serve in the military, you should be required to shave your head bald regardless of any military branch that you serve in! The people in power who establish laws in the military should enforce this order and stop being sexist themselves towards men. This is not about being a gentleman, but serving in the military is a matter of life and death; and if women will continue to refuse shaving their head bald and serving in front-line infantry battalions/regiments, then do not deserve equal rights as men!

Female Privileges in America!
Exposing Feminist Hypocrisy!

VI

-Always Girl's night out advertisements from clubs, where women receive free entrance and discounts on drinks but never boys night out advertisements where men receive discounts for entrance (yet alone free entrance) to a club and drinks like women receive-

This is basic observation and common sense for every man who took out a woman on a date to a club and/or bar. Not all clubs/bars endorse this practice/policy or even practice free admission to women and discounts on drinks for women, but plenty of them do all across the United States. Why? Because, the owners and managers of these bars and clubs desire to establish special privleges to women because either they view these women as superior to men, or should be treated superior because their inferior to men. There cannot be a third option. Ultimately, the primary yet reasonable practice for this is to establish revenue and profit for the business, because most men realize and understand that women are naive when under the influence of either alcohol and/or drugs. They will fall for anything so long as they can be convinced that what you're saying to them is the truth but also in which they agree with. Regardless, imagine if there were only signs all across clubs and bars that stated "Men get in for free, girls have to pay $10.00 admission?" Feminist women would probably protest

Female Privileges in America!
Exposing Feminist Hypocrisy!

against these measures because to them, this is unequal treatment towards them, in the same way that it's unequal treatment towards men. It's no different from charging a black man $10.00 dollars to enter a club, and yet allowing a white person to get in for free. Somehow, someway, I guess feminists never challenge these practices because it does not apply to them, and if they really did care for equal treatment for both genders, (Male and Female), they would also include this unfair treatment against men; but they don't because feminists are hypocrites. Feminists only complain when they do not receive things or entitlements in their favor. However, this clearly violates the 1964 Civil Rights Act signed into law by President Lyndon Baines Johnson which clearly states that:

Congress passed Public Law 88-352 (78 Stat. 241). The Civil Rights Act of 1964 prohibits discrimination on the basis of race, color, religion, sex or national origin. Provisions of this civil rights act forbade discrimination on the basis of sex, as well as, race in hiring, promoting, and firing. The Act prohibited discrimination in public accommodations and federally funded programs. It also strengthened the enforcement of voting rights and the desegregation of schools.

It's ironic that this bill was signed into law by a Democratic president, and yet most liberal feminists who are primarily democrats choose and intentionally select to ignore these rights that should be practiced, but again, these liberal-democratic-feminist women only seek benefits from our

Female Privileges in America!
Exposing Feminist Hypocrisy!

beautiful nation and not the responsibilities that our nation requires them to engage in. The responsibility consists of paying a fee to enter a club and/or bar at the same price as men. America will never see one, and I mean one feminist woman, ever protest for this unfair treatment established against men. Why? Because feminists are not for humanity, but rather for their own gender; and they do not desire equal treatment as men allegedly receive; in which I have illustrated multiple examples throughout this book that currently men do not receive in A.D, 2022; but rather feminists desire and demand superior treatmentand in return, yet they will deliver not enough labor, creations, discoveries, inventions, ideas, as men have established throughout history; and will continue to do as centuries pass. If you really think about it, after all the houses, buildings, cars, electrical poles, and other things that men assembled, why the hell do men not receive free admission and discounts as women receive at these institutions? The answer for this is men who have either never been betrayed by women or been manipulated by them from their actions; and instead have followed their mothers advice to "always be a gentleman towards women" which is another definition of being an utter yet complete dumbass-submissive man towards women is the reason why the United States of America is going down. Somehow, someway, no thanks to the liberal-feminist media, women have been taught to believe that they can be brave, patriotic, daring, and engage in physical labor such as men and yet most if not all women reject all of these jobs that require excessive responsibility and physical labor. For the record, nurses who clean feces off of patients from patients at

Female Privileges in America!
Exposing Feminist Hypocrisy!

hospitals is not necessarily physical labor and if you think it is, men also engage in this practice. For women who think that raising children is physical labor, it's not entirely, and also men engage in this practice as well. Where is the father's appreciation? Why is this topic brought up in this paragraph? Because, many children are conceived from either one or both parents being intoxicated from a night of drinking or at a night club/bar or at home drinking. It's fair to say that most children are not planned in the United States yet alone on planet Earth! But the point is that there should be an ending towards special and convenient treatment towars women; because so long as they believe that they will always receive special and superior treatment above men, than they will take steps to manipulate and take advantage of men when and if that man that they're dating is vulnerable and ignorant. We must stop this mentality from feminists and blood-sucking women who desire to trap men for their own financial benefits. Let this chapter be a reminder to all men that women can easily be predators as men. A predator may not always be a person who takes life, but also robs someone of financial stability in which women consistently do to men. Let every reader reading this remember that! Do not make the same mistake as many men made before you regardless of how good the sex is that the woman that you're with gives you currently today. It's just a mask and an addictive poison to lure you towards her so she can control your life and expenses; in favor of her personal expenses. You must always assume that no matter how nice that your girlfriend or wife is to you, that she will either cheat, steal, and manipulate you to be someone else in order to establish her

Female Privileges in America!
Exposing Feminist Hypocrisy!

own personal desires. You must never obey or accept these requests for your own personal economical circumstances and advantages; and also for your own personal pride. Pride is important for every man. Pride must never be compromised, overlooked, and/or rejected by anybody, no woman, and no man on Earth; regardless of love, sex, benefits, and/or money! Pride is important and essential to establish proper meaning and points; and to also correct the idiots who are wrong who believe that they're correct but ultimately wrong because those are the people (the feminists & socialist Democrats) who complain about many dillusional arguements but can never establish credibility on behalf of their arguements. If you really think about, feminists act like socialists in which they believe "that they all deserve equal treatment for the work/actions that they performed." In other words, women expect men to pay for them and their expenses regardless if these women worked or not for them. To them, because they're women, they deserve and expect equal treatment and equal distribution. Does this not sound alot like women asking for benefits when a marriage is no longer suitable for them? Does this also not sound like a man who has paid for everything (dates, engagement rings, rent, mortgages, insurance bills, groceries, clothes) is not entitled to reimbursement because he's a man. That's his obligation at least according to women. Be responsible and pay your bills on time, yet they don't have too because they have or rely on you to pay for them even though these women do not work and/or refuse to work! That to me, sounds a lot like socialism. An individual who is lazy or refusing to get their hands dirty and work hard, assumes or expects that he or she

Female Privileges in America!
Exposing Feminist Hypocrisy!

should receive payments just because she's married to you and breathes oxygen. This is the result of dating which may in many cases lead to marriage. This is similar to socialism in which "wealth is distrubuted to people regardless if they worked hard or not from the company or in cases of marriage." A lot of women after getting married, stop cooking, cleaning, and doing chores around their own household for their men. Neither of these are fair systems and they don't work either; otherwise American women and people from all across the planet would go to socialist countries instead of attempting to smuggle themselves here in the United States. The truth is, is that women know that they benefit the most from living in the United States and yet complain about it's policies and procedures; and the only reason why is because the majority of feminists are either dillusional or suffer from multiple mental illnesses because after all the proof that I described in this book about women receiving better and superior treatment than men in this country, still continues to be overlooked and intentionally ignored; and this can only indictate biased, stupidity, ignorance, and/or mental illness (delusions) that men in somehow, someway, receive better treatment than women in the United States. I do not agree with that. I personally agree that feminists generally exhibit hatred towards men, and yet enjoy all of the inventions and discoveries that men has achieved up into today, that these same feminists also enjoy and take advantage of today themselves. The hypocrisy of feminism speaks for itself; just like a man who has to pay a fee to enter a club or bar and yet his date who is generally a woman gets in for free. That's bullshit if you ask me. The

Female Privileges in America!
Exposing Feminist Hypocrisy!

woman should have to pay for her own entrance regardless if the man asked her out for a date. It's all about equality right? Yet, many women will argue that "he asked me out, he should pay for everything!" A better question remains is "if women are so equal to men, why don't they ask men out for dates? If women are equal today to men, why do men have to practice traditional values (asking women out and paying for their expenses) and yet women still enjoy the convenient benefits as they always have througout history and never have to ask men out for dates?" The reason why again is because women from all races and from all ages, want the benefits but not the responsibilites as a traditional woman. They feel as if they're entitled and superior. Otherwise, they would ask men out for dates. Right? Unless women are cheap and not generous to ask men out! This could be another logical reason on why women do not ask men out. Generally, it's no secret that women are cheap and desire to never spend anything on a man unless it's to manipulate him to marrying her; but generally, women expect men to pay for their personal finances and expenses.

VII

–Women pay less than men for car insurance-

Yes, it's hard to believe that even sexism against men also exists in the insurance world; despite the fact that insurance

Female Privileges in America!
Exposing Feminist Hypocrisy!

companies are supposed to not discriminate against either men or women. Men invented all brands of vehicles, and yet still pay more insurance premuims than women who have never invented any brand of a vehicle. Sounds fair right? Before we continue my argument on why men should not have to pay more car insurance than women for the same year and same make and model for a car, let's first demonstrate some facts so feminists can't say shit about me intentionally ignoring other facts directly or indirectly related to men paying more for car insurance at least according to these accurate studies, data, and publications:

The National Highway Traffic Safety Administration reports that men cause an average of 6.1 million accidents per year in the U.S., and women cause 4.4 million accidents per year. According to the Insurance Information Institute, male drivers were responsible for 37,477 fatal crashes while women were responsible for 13,502 fatal accidents in 2017. These statistics tend to support the assertion that men are worse drivers than women. However, examining the data further reveals some additional facts.

According to the University of Michigan Transportation Research Institute, 104.3 million men 105.7 million women in the U.S. have drivers' licenses. The Federal Highway Administration reports that men drive an average of 16,550 miles each year. Women drive an average of 10,142 miles per year, demonstrating that women drive much less than men on average. When taken together, these statistics demonstrate that women drive 30% less than men do on an annual basis. While men cause more accidents than women, women have a slightly higher risk of being involved in accidents per mile driven.

Female Privileges in America!
Exposing Feminist Hypocrisy!

Which Gender Pays More for Car Insurance?

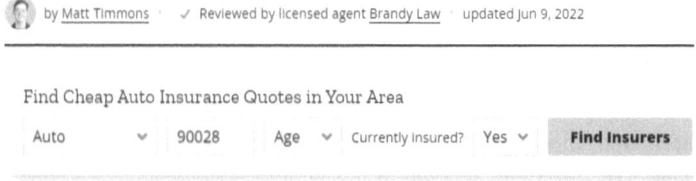 by Matt Timmons · ✓ Reviewed by licensed agent Brandy Law · updated Jun 9, 2022

Find Cheap Auto Insurance Quotes in Your Area

| Auto | 90028 | Age | Currently insured? | Yes | **Find Insurers** |

In most states, car insurance companies are allowed to consider your gender when setting car insurance rates. Over the course of their lifetimes, women tend to pay slightly less — but only by a small amount. Younger men and women will see the biggest gender gap, while adult drivers can typically expect a price difference between men and women of less than 1%.

- Who pays more for car insurance, men or women?
- Age affects the insurance cost gap between genders
- Some states don't permit gender to impact insurance rates

Who pays more for car insurance, men or women?

Female Privileges in America!
Exposing Feminist Hypocrisy!

Which gender pays more for car insurance?

Teenage boys pay more for insurance than teenage girls, but the price gap narrows as drivers age.

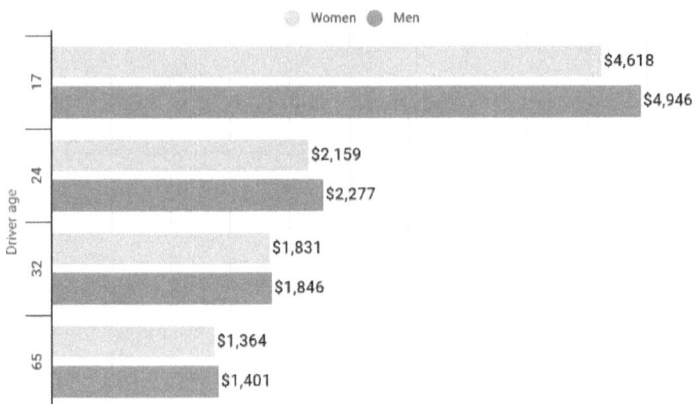

Age	Women	Men	Percentage difference
17	$4,618	$4,946	-6.6%
24	$2,159	$2,277	-5.2%
32	$1,831	$1,846	-0.8%
65	$1,364	$1,401	-2.6%

Why do men pay more for car insurance?

Insurance companies don't explain directly why one group of people pays more for car insurance than another. But in general, insurers charge more for people who are statistically more likely to be involved in an accident or make a claim on their policy.

In other words, insurers have found that **boys and young men are more likely to get in car accidents than other people** — even more than young women. Young men may be more likely to purchase a sports car, speed or take risks behind the wheel.

142

Female Privileges in America!
Exposing Feminist Hypocrisy!

Some states don't permit gender to impact insurance rates

There are a few states that explicitly forbid insurance companies from considering gender when it comes to insurance rates. Those states are:

- California
- Hawaii
- Massachusetts
- Michigan
- Montana
- North Carolina
- Pennsylvania

If you live in one of these states, your insurer cannot take your gender into consideration when setting rates — in most cases, the insurer won't even ask.

CBS News reports that men are also much likelier than women to be cited for reckless driving. According to that study, men have a 3.1% greater chance of being ticketed for reckless driving than women.

While women may be less likely to engage in risky driving behaviors and drive fewer miles than men each year, there are several reasons why they have a slightly higher risk of accidents for each mile driven in a year than men. Since they drive fewer miles, they have less experience with navigating the dangers of the roads. Women also tend to be shorter than men, and they may have more trouble seeing oncoming vehicles when they are completing turns because of visual obstacles. Previously, there was a larger gap between the accident risks among younger drivers. However, that gap has been closing as more girls are driving while they are distracted by their cell phones. A study by the Insurance Journal found that females of all ages are much likelier to use their cell phones while they drive than men.

Here are the facts based on these studies and data as I mentioned earlier.
- *Men typically get more involved in car collisions than women.*
- *Men drive more than women due to multiple reasons involving work and other tasks despite the fact that women in the United States are primary license holders than men. More women own driver licenses than men, yet men drive more.*

Female Privileges in America!
Exposing Feminist Hypocrisy!

- *Men pay more car insurance than women because of the assumed belief that eventually every man who drives will crash into someone somehow, someway in which the man driving would be at fault. As a result, the insurance worker is compelled or trained to intentionally charge men more money as a condition for men to operate their vehicles.*
- *Allegedly, there are no gender discrimination in certain states (California, Hawaii, Massachusetts, Michigan, Montana, North Carolina, and Pennsylvania) because it's prohibited. I don't even think feminists believe in this nonsense!*
- *Women are not necessarily driving experts when driving through dangerous roads in which may include extreme weather conditions.*
- *Women are more typically shorter than men and therfore sometimes have trouble yielding on the road because they can't see incoming traffic (excuses).*
- *Women are more focused talking on their cell phones while driving, than driving defensively than men; and is increasing their traffic collisions potentially reaching equally or higher rates of traffic collisions as men today.*

So far these are the facts based on studies and observations from The National Highway Traffic Safety Administration among other websites confirming such information and studies. This whole argument goes back to the points that I made earlier in my previous chapters which include the following:

Female Privileges in America!
Exposing Feminist Hypocrisy!

- *Men are more ambitious than women to travel to and from work at longer distances than women. This might explain the reason for higher traffic collisions engaged by men than women.*
- *Men risk their safety much more than women in order to get their priorities and agendas completed; which is why men drive more miles than women, and crash more than women.*
- *Women are given special and superior treatment than men in all circumstances which is the judicial system, work environments, education facilities, dates (they rarely pay for anything), girls night out discounts at clubs, and much more. So, why would women also not receive special treatment from insurance companies if they receive superior treatment from almost everything else that they receive in the United States?*
- *Women probably rely on men to pick them up for dates or other tasks, so they can save themselves gas and mileage if their vehicle is leased. Note: Leased vehicles can only be driven a certain amount of miles annually before being overcharged; unlike a purchased vehicle with monthly payments where you can waste as many miles as you wan't. That's basic car dealership 101.*
- *Women probably have the belief or notion that men should stop for them while driving, even if it's the man's right away (the woman is in a yielding lane) because men should be gentleman even on the streets. Note: I actually believe this theory to be sometimes accurate*

Female Privileges in America!
Exposing Feminist Hypocrisy!

based on my personal experience driving where women have expected me to stop for them or they will cross across traffic forcing everyone to stop for them so they can make a u-turn on streets. I'm sure every man reading this has had this happen to them while they were driving at some point in their life.

- *It's implausible for me to believe that an exotic looking woman, dressed in attention-seeking attire who walks into a car insurance agency to purchase car insurance from a pointdexter-looking guy, will have to pay the same amount of car insurance for the same brand/year and make and model of a vehicle, that an obese unattractive looking man who wants to purchase the same insurance for the same brand/year and make and model of a car will have to pay from the same pointdexter looking guy. I believe that if both the exotic woman and obese unattractive man never had any history of car accidents and are the same age, that the exotic woman will somehow, someway get a discount for looking good while the obese unattractive man will probably pay just a little bit more, because after all, he's a man. Unless pointdexter's gay, then there might be a different scenario. The point is, is that car insurance agencies are biased against men when making quotations for car insurance rates for men, compared to women. Insurance agents may be prohibited in California and Montana from openly admitting that "because you're a man, you have to pay more insurance*

Female Privileges in America!
Exposing Feminist Hypocrisy!

rates because men crash more than women." They know if they say shit like this, you're just going to get up from your seat and walk away which loses business and profit for these insurance companies. However, the insurance agents can think and do as they well please. They just can't be biased against genders verbally or establish some proof that the insurance agent is intentionally overcharging a man because of his gender. Are we to believe that insurance agents honorably set higher insurance rates for men who have no history of car accidents because it's an accident? No, I don't believe that! Are we to believe that women get cheaper car insurance rates than men because women are less likely to crash more than men? Yes and no! Yes, because a woman may have no history of car accidents, and no because women generally are used to at least in the United States of America of receiving discounts, benefits, and superior treatment when compared to men who receive not even close to the same treatment as women. There is an additional point that I would like to mention in this chapter in which I do not understand why car insurance agencies do not also include the fact that women may be a threat or danger to other drivers on streets, highways, and/or freeways because if their vehicle breaks down suddenly, a vehicle can rear-end them from behind or from the side. Yes, while it's true that "acts of nature" do happen where cars break down suddenly, televisions stop turning on, and a refrigerator might break down over time, cars can be maintained by

Female Privileges in America!
Exposing Feminist Hypocrisy!

their owners. Women however, almost never maintain their vehicles. You will almost never see a woman put oil, power steering fluid, coolant, or even brake fluid inside their vehicles. Why? Because their lazy or entitled to expect someone else to do it for them (usually a boyfriend or husband or other male friend). I will give an example of this. If a woman drives an older-generation vehicle and it has an oil leak, and chooses not to put engine oil or fix her oil-pan-gasket to prevent the leak of oil, eventually her engine will burn and be destroyed. If this happens, her car can stop suddenly in the middle of a road, highway, and/or freeway putting other people's lives in danger for her negligence. Regardless if she needed transportation to get to work, school, or pick up her kids, she should not be driving a vehicle that is unreliable and potentially dangerous towards other people on the road. Men generally maintain their vehicles and take care of them; at least a hell of a lot more than women, I'll tell you that much. But for some reason, insurance agencies know this, but does not take into account the reality that women demonstrate poor judgement more than men when maintaining vehicles which is essential and necessary to prevent car accidents. The same goes for an inflated tire. If a woman knows that she needs to put air in her tire and somehow believes that the problem will fix itself, eventually when she's driving, the tire will give out, in which she will not have total control of the vehicle, and the vehicle may (after swerving and cutting

Female Privileges in America!
Exposing Feminist Hypocrisy!

across many people in order to avoid crashing) just crash into someone or something. Observance and inspections of your vehicle is necessary and important for both genders (this includes non-binary people who are still confused about their gender and can't make up their mind what gender they are) to practice driving defensively regardless whether they do it themselves, or pay someone else to do it for them. If that is not proof enough of how women feel privleged and entitled NOT to learn any information of the car that they operate then let's take a look at this article which was written by a woman herself (surprisingly).

Lori Johnson is really good at being a fly on the wall. During her 31 years as a Pennsylvania-based automotive technician, she's had the opportunity to observe some pretty interesting behaviours.

Like the time she was completing her undergraduate degree in Women's Studies and Sociology and writing a research paper on how women are treated in automotive stores. To find out, she asked an auto parts store if she could just hang out for the day. Without telling the employees what she was up to, Johnson watched. Did women beeline it for the counter and ask a technician for help, or did they look around for a while and try to find the part themselves?

"Women tended to ask questions and go right up to the counter," she recalls. "They didn't know where to look and they didn't really know what they were looking for."

Then there was the time Johnson was working at a Honda dealership and helped teach an informational class to new car buyers, both male and female. During one of the classes, she took a step back and noticed that the men were super involved but the women weren't really engaged.

"They were taking notes feverishly in the back," says Johnson, "but they weren't asking questions."

Johnson's anecdotes are revealing. Women don't want to look silly in front of men around cars — and as a result, won't take steps to educate themselves. But what does this intimidation cost them?

For the record, this article was written by Lisa Coxon! A woman who confirms that women in general in the United States are very ignorant or stupid about understanding cars and how they operate. All that women desire is to drive the vehicle and when mechanicle problems occur, they believe, feel, and

Female Privileges in America!
Exposing Feminist Hypocrisy!

expect men to fix their problems for them so these same women who require the ability to drive again, rely on men to resolve their problems (both mechanically and financially). It would be so entertaining to see these feminist women fix their own vehicles or walk miles and miles on end to reach their destination but of course, they will never accept or expect this treatment like women did centuries ago. Feminist women, although they say that they can do the work as a man, such as being a mechanic, contradicts their claims because "when the hell again do you see female mechanics in the United States unless their butch lesbians?" Feminists demand and expect equal pay for equal work but will limit themselves and set their own standards so they will not get their hands dirty. This mentality and behavior is typical of a liberal Democrat or socialist who think that their superior above everyone else in this country and therfore should not have to wash dishes in a restaurant or clean restrooms or be a maid because their mentality is, "I'm smarter than everyone else I wen't to a university. I should never have to clean up after anyone elses mess!" No wonder why these stupid liberal Democrats wan't immigrans here in California, so that immigrants can do the dirty work for Democrats and liberals, but yet never obtain the same respect and hospitality as white liberal democrats treat each other. This is pure hypocriosy from the left wing and liberal Democrats In-general. It would be nice to see a white liberal woman change her own tire, or be a mechanic

Female Privileges in America!
Exposing Feminist Hypocrisy!

but most women will never do this because again it goes back to "double standards." It's a man's job (whether he is a Democrat or Republican) to inspect and fix cars!" But when you ask a young woman to cook or clean for you, the typical response is, "this is not the 1950's anymore. Women are smart and leaders and do not answer to you." Any woman that tells you this, do not even bother dating or marrying her yet alone knowing her. She's garbage and will only ruin your financial circumstances and agendas. Beware of her bullshit! This is for your own financial safety and the opportunity to eliminate any potential financial, emotional, and physical stress that a woman that you settle down with will deliver to you. Trust the author of this book, when he mentions this: **THE PUSSY IS NOT WORTH IT! NO MATTER HOW MANY HOLES (ORAL, VAGINAL, AND/OR ANAL) SHE GIVES YOU OR POSITIONS THAT SHE GIVES TO YOU, IT'S ALL AN ACT TO TRAP YOU SO THAT SHE CAN ROB YOU FINANCIALLY YET LEGALLY (THROUGH THE COURT SYSTEMS WHETHER OR NOT YOU MARRY HER).**

In reponse to losing all of your money potentially to a coniving, selfish, and narcissistic woman, just use her, before she tries to use you. Women these days, in our modern times are not worth your time, effort, money, and/or loyalty. American women will use and take advantage of you only to benefit themselves while

Female Privileges in America!
Exposing Feminist Hypocrisy!

impressing their friends and family. The exception to the rule for some women who will not use you, still does apply, but why risk your chances? Why bankrupt yourself for a selfish broad who is so prideful and potentially vindictive towards you? The risk is not worth it! Be careful and look out for your own financial circumstances because women, generally will never invest in anything that you wan't or desire unless they get a share out of it (which is generally a lifetime amount of money given towards them) and yet they will expect you to invest in them and in their expenses. That is not a man's priority or obligation; and the more men do this, the more that American women will naturally accept and embrace this "entitled privelege." We have to stop this, because we must demonstrate and show an example that women are not superior to men, and also do not generally deserve special treatment (opening doors for them, paying their bills, and tolerating their bullshit) from men today. The sooner that men stop giving in to these demands from women, the sooner that women will begin to realize that their not superior to men or deserve certain special treatment just because they have a vagina. We men, must unite and stop being gentleman towards women and stop giving women the impression that "we can't live without them." Pride is an important and valuable thing for a man, and we must practice our personal pride against women in the United States of America where women are given everything and anything above men. We must reverse this practice

Female Privileges in America!
Exposing Feminist Hypocrisy!

and permantely change it in favor of men being in charge of their own lives and destiny!

VIII

-Require DNA testing from women who are allegedly pregnant with your child-

Female Privileges in America!
Exposing Feminist Hypocrisy!

Paternity Fraud: Top 3 Reasons Why Some Mother's May Lie.

Have you ever been accused of being the biological father of a child and later you found out you were not? Or, do you know someone (friend or family) that has gone through this experience? If you answered yes to these questions, I am sure you probably wondered why would any woman do this to the alleged father. In this post, we will list the explanation given by women we have encountered over the years performing a DNA Test.

Below is a list of reasons some women have given to why they knowingly made her decision to commit Paternity Fraud. The list is not in any particular order of frequency.

1. Financial stability – The biological father was considered to be an irresponsible person.
2. Alleged Father was easier to communicate with.
3. Fear of ruining her relationship

This chapter is important and a reminder to feminists that although men may use women for a night of cheap sex after a date, it's nothing compared to a woman using men for 18 years (if not more additional years) to pay for a child that is not biologically his. Yet, some cowardly women, out of fear of losing financial stability and in order to gain financial stability (to benefit themselves) intentionally lie to men or do everything they can to convince the man that she personally selected to be the father of a child that is not biologically his. Although the man did sleep with her, the woman quizzes this as an advantage to demonstrate deception that she was impregnated by a man that she probably only has interest in because of his money; and would prefer that man to be the real father (even though he's not biologically) than the asshole that she slept with previously but would prefer not to be with because of that asshole's financial irresponsibility. Again it goes back to the concept and ideology that women "ONLY WANT MONEY FROM MEN!" They don't give a shit about anybody but themselves and their financial circumstances. Generally, most women are this way, but

Female Privileges in America!
Exposing Feminist Hypocrisy!

again their is a few out there who actually have some values. But the point of this chapter is to encourage men to always request a DNA test if you're girlfriend or wife is pregnant with your child based on her words. She may or probably throw a fit and an argument against you but it's to your financial benefit. Women lie all the time. Men do as well but generally when men lie, they don't get away with it. Women always do because when they cry, and pretend to be a victim; they make the perfect actresses. What's worse, is people for that shit. If you ever see the television show "COPS" you will know what I mean because almost all men who are being either detained or arrested never cry, and yet almost all women who are being detained or arrested almost always cry. Crying is always generaly a character of expressing your weak side. Men don't cry often because they have to deal with so much bullshit that generally women don't have to deal with. Anyway, the article posted in this chapter should be a reminder to men that women can easily tell you that "she's pregnant with your child" but in fact she can be pregnant with someone else's child. To ensure your financial safety, ALWAYS GET A DNA TEST TO PROVE THAT YOU'RE THE FATHER! If you have ever seen paternity court or Maury (you're not the father episodes), I strongly suggest that you watch them and also watch and be aware of your girlfriend or wife's actions. Because if you're not careful, you will become a victim, and the courts will not give a shit about what you wan't or think.

Female Privileges in America!
Exposing Feminist Hypocrisy!

Remember most of the judges in every court across this country are baby boomers. These men grew up in different times; where their mothers and women that they dated were a lot more potentially genuine and caring; therfore, they cannot see the flaw in women today who are almost the complete opposite of the women that they grew up with during their time. Although, they may give sentences to younger women, in these young generations, it's very different to observe someones actions, and be put in their shoes. A lot of these old ass judges have never been put in a pair of shoes of dealing with selfish and prideful women. Don't believe me? Look at their current marriage records. Now why do I bring this up? Because dome dumb ass male judges (and some women judges too) will force a man to pay for a child that is not his, because the mother is complaining and demanding money from the man in a court. Some judges are fair and will reject this nonsense and other's are stupid asses and actually know full well that the alleged father is not the biological father, and yet will still require the man who is not the father to pay child support regardless if he's challenging the idea that he has to pay because he's not the father. What's even more important to remember and understand is this same posting and publication listed on this chapter:

Female Privileges in America!
Exposing Feminist Hypocrisy!

If a mother lies on a birth certificate can she be sued in court?

To my knowledge mothers are not often prosecuted for lying knowingly about the paternity of her child. The issue here is actually providing proof that the mother intentionally committed fraud.

Can I sue for lying about paternity?

If a legal father wants to sue the mother of his alleged child misattributing paternity. We recommend first consulting with an attorney in your state to get advice about how your state handles this issue. If you are unable to afford an attorney. Then I suggest you research the paternity laws in your state to learn more about your rights and the possibility of suing a mother for misattributing paternity.

So if a father refuses to pay child support, he can go to jail and some fathers have with good reason. The author does believe that biological fathers should be their for his or her children and also contribute financially towards his offspring. However, if women lie about misleading men to pay for her bullshit which is sleeping with different men (which is not a mistake because unless she was raped, she choose to practice her slutty behavior) somehow, someway, she is excluded from criminal prosecution because the law states, "that there must be proof that she intentionally committed fraud." What court or judge, or prosecutor would even look into this or consider this? Especially if these people are voted into their positions by their constituents, knowing full well that that any act against women would potentially lose votes for them in any electrion. It may also not be a voting concept. It could be that these people (judges and prosecutors) cannot believe that a woman would lie about something so heinous, such as getting pregnant and refusing to have an abortion, that

Female Privileges in America!
Exposing Feminist Hypocrisy!

these judges will side in the woman's favor. After all, think about this. It's evil but genius. Get yourself pregnant, pretend to be pro-life, and cry in court and make yourslef look like a victim; and that's all that takes is for an idiot judge to automatically think that the man who is allegedly the father of her child (who really isn't) will make him pay for that child. It's unfair and immoral. Again, to avoid these circumstances, always request a DNA test regardless of how defensive that your girlfriend or wife will be. If she is defensive, you should also reconsider continuing to live with her or even marrying her, if she is just your girlfriend; because if she has nothing to hide, why would she be so angry to agree to a DNA test? It's best to ask yourself these questions! It's important towards your financial stability! Fuck her financial stability!

Can a DNA test be done without the mother?

This is a two-fold answer. If you want to know if you are the father for informational purposes only. Then the answer is yes. This type of paternity test is known as a peace of mind DNA test. Remember, this type of test cannot be used in court.

In the event, you would like to use a DNA result for legal purposes the alleged father would have to have his name on the birth certificate in order to perform a legal DNA test without the mother's consent. As it currently stands in most, If not all states. This applies only to unmarried men. Married men automatically are deemed custodial parents and can make decisions for the child. Therefore the courts would deem the result admissible.

Please note, it is not recommended that you perform a DNA test with the mother if are not on good communicating terms. Because, If the DNA test result is submitted and used in court and the mother was not present for the sample collection. It is almost certain the judge will grant the mother's request that you perform another DNA test. If the mother refuses, I suggest that you petition the court in your state and have the judge issue a court order to force the mother to partake in DNA testing.

Men, are you reading this? A "piece of mind DNA test" is basically useless against you in court. Then of course,

Female Privileges in America!
Exposing Feminist Hypocrisy!

never forget that you need to have your name on the birth certificate that is allegedly your child without the mother's consent! This generally applies only to unmarried men! Married men are automatically fucked as they're deemed to be custodial parents. According to this article if your girlfriend or wife is pissed off at you, and you demand a DNA test from her for her to provide proof to you that you're the biological father of her child; and she's not present to provide a DNA sample, then the judge will still be on her side and request that you come back again to demand a DNA sample. In other words, you're time is not important and and your time is worthless but the woman's time is valuable and priceless. In many cases, many men have to petition the court to provide a DNA testing from the mother. If the mother could not make it to court (unless it's an emergency) what does she have to hide?

Female Privileges in America!
Exposing Feminist Hypocrisy!

ST. AUGUSTINE, Fla. — Joseph Sinawa feels like he's fighting an uphill battle against the state of Florida. He's being forced to pay child support despite a DNA test proving he is not the biological father.

"I signed the birth certificate because at the time I believed I was the biological father," said Sinawa.

He says the child's mother is even okay with him not paying child support because she doesn't want anything to do with him, but the state is forcing the issue.

"She told the judge she just wants this to be done and over with, and so do I," he says.

On top of it all, Sinawa says he struggled when he learned the child was not his.

"I was emotionally devastated," he said.

Carnell Alexander is not the father of the now-adult child for whom several courts, including the Wayne County Circuit Court this week, have ordered him to pay $30,000 in back child support for. How do we know he's not the father? Because he took a DNA test proving the contrary, and even the mother (an ex-girlfriend) now says he's not.

Female Privileges in America!
Exposing Feminist Hypocrisy!

How is it possible in the Land of the Free that men can face huge fines, revocation of professional licenses, forfeiture of the right to international travel, and sometimes (as in Alexander's case until this week) even jail time, from owing child support to kids that aren't theirs? I wrote a feature about that 11 years ago, entitled "Injustice by Default." Short version:

Governments (and sometimes even hospitals) are financially incentivized to attach paternity to the children of single mothers, particularly those seeking welfare benefits. Departments of Child Support Services will sometimes go on information as flimsy as "Dude with this name living in Southern California"; if a records search turns up only one dude, he will likely be mailed a court summons. That court summons will often be very confusingly written, so that the men don't realize that they are just 30 days away from being declared the father via default judgment. Once you have been named the father, you owe all back child support (sometimes with interest), said support will be garnished from your wages, and it is devilishly hard to get your paternity undeclared, even with DNA proof and sworn affidavits from the mother.

Carnell Alexander is one example of many men who have been deceived by women but also forced to pay for these women's children by a court of law. Here is another example of an innocent man who was defrauded from a woman but yet neglected in a court of law from a judge who decided to be sexist and side in favor of a woman despite being required to uphold the law and practice justice. The only thing that these judges practice is sexist, flawed, and superior treatment towards women who are using men financially because they fucked up their own lives and refuse to fix it themselves!

Female Privileges in America!
Exposing Feminist Hypocrisy!

Man ordered to pay $65K in child support for kid who isn't his

By Fox News   July 23, 2017 | 7:39pm | Updated

ORIGINALLY PUBLISHED BY:

Teachers union not backing bill nixing teacher-student sex

Tennessee judge rules gay couples have equal parental rights

A Texas man is battling a court order that mandates he must pay tens of thousands in child support for a child whom he did not biologically father and whom he met only once.

In 2003, a child support court in Texas ruled that Gabriel Cornejo, 45, had to pay child support to his ex-girlfriend, who had recently given birth, because she vowed there was no way he wasn't the rightful dad.

Cornejo, who is currently raising three children of his own and two nephews, claimed he was not made aware of this and only found out about the child support payments last year when a deputy served him with court papers claiming that the state of Texas lists him as having another child. He soon met the minor for the first and only time — describing her as a "wonderful girl" — but after taking a DNA test, learned she was not his after all.

Only Cornejo's ex-girlfriend and the state still want the $65,000 in back payments.

"I never thought in my whole life I would have to defend myself of something that I am innocent of," he said

The reality and the truth is, is that a lot of men are being lied to by women that they slept with to be a father to a child that is not theirs. The mainstream media almost never reports this because it would destroy the credibility of the average American woman. However, these articles published in this book, is just a few of many unresolved circumstances of men that are battling the courts to not be forced to pay money to women for a child that they (the women) claim is his, but is actually not! Isn't it sad, how the news and the media criticize men for refusing to be a part of their childs life and

Female Privileges in America!
Exposing Feminist Hypocrisy!

provide financially for his son and/or daughter and yet never once on the news (on television) are women ever criticized for their deception of trying to trap a man to pay for a child that isn't his. Many men have cried and have been emotionally destroyed not so much for the financial payments, but also being lied to by his girlfriend or wife that the child that he has helped raised is not his. Again, some women don't give a shit about these men's feelings. They only give a shit about the money that they can receive from the man. This chapter alone proves beyond a reasonable doubt that women benefit more in society, the media, and the judicial system because of their gender and not their opinions, thoughts, feelings, and/or actions. It's truly sad. The only response for men to counter potential deceptive behavior from women is to always wear condoms, and demand a DNA test. Who knows? Maybe a judge will be in your favor if some bitch lies about you impregnating her when in fact another man did. Always try to check her cell phone too because she may be texting the father of her child or be sleeping with someone else; and if she refuses, always record this by any means necessary, and refuse to continue to date and/or sleep with her because she cannot be trusted and probably will betray you when your back is turned. It's a risk that you cannot take and in these economical times, every dollar that you make belongs to you and not to some bitch who will take advantage of you!

Female Privileges in America!
Exposing Feminist Hypocrisy!

-The Conclusion-

In the end, it's youre choice. Many of you men reading this last chapter or earlier chapters will naturally make your own final testaments and decisions. Some of you will ignore and resent my arguments without providing any debates and/or arguments because your current girlfriends and wives have been so kind and reasonable towards you. You may not see the evil, deception and flawed personality in women either because your girlfriend and/or wife has given you everything from giving you sex, cooking and cleaning for you, and/or picking you up from work and/or raising your children. But always understand this. NOTHING IS FREE IN LIFE! Women do not do this out of the kindness of their heart (generally), they do these actions for you because they expect something and in some cases everything in return. Our mothers do not ever teach us men how women treat and expect from men but rather try or at least attempt their sons on how to treat women which is complete bullshit. How I was raised by my mother, was "be a gentleman towards a woman." Now, exactly what does that mean being a gentleman? Bring flowers? Open the door for your date/girlfriend/wife, pay her bills, pay for dates, pick her up in your car and take her back home (if she does not live with you)? That to me sounds like a simp and an idiot. Women in these modern times do not deserve these special treatments because they never reciprocate this same gratitude and attitude

Female Privileges in America!
Exposing Feminist Hypocrisy!

towards men. Instead, modern American women are only focused on trying to impress their family on how much of a rich man she has been able to reel in compared to her friends and/or family as if it's such a competition. This is why it's best to avoid these circumstances and follow your instinct and gut-reaction. Women can be as evil as men but unlike men, who rarely get away with their actions, women can get away their actions because of their gender. If this is a game, don't even bother rolling the dice, just walk away and never tolerate her bullshit. Living with women only brings misery to men because of their high demands and expectations. Always remember men, that all it takes is that when you live with a woman and she calls the police because both of you had an argument, YOU'RE AT SUCH RISK OF BEING ARRESTED FOR DOMESTIC VIOLENCE EVEN IF SHE HITS YOU FIRST AND YOU PUSH HER AWAY FROM YOU! If this does happen to you, and you're convicted of domestic violence, you're life is over for generally 4-7 years depending on the state that you live for jobs that do background checks on you; regardless if it's a misdemeanor or felony. Beware always, and if you're girlfriend or wife physically abuses you, you're not being a pussy for calling the police, you're only defending yourself and your financial circumstances because if you fail to report this, she will only continue this behavior and more than likely your local law enforcement department will not believe you. Establish a

Female Privileges in America!
Exposing Feminist Hypocrisy!

record of your girlfriend or wife attempting to provoke you to hit her, so you have an alibi against her. If you do not do this, no police department will ever believe you or take your side; if something does go down where you and your girlfriend or wife got into a verbal and/or physical confrontation, a suggestion for you could be is to put hiddien cameras in your apartment and/or house that you both reside in, so that could establish evidence in a court of law. In the end, it's your choice, but because we live in the 21st century, the entire United States of America is generally in favor of women's rights instead of men's rights. For all those feminists reading this final chapter, you will continue to believe in your delusional concept that somehow, someway, you're a victim and given inferior treatment when compared to men's treatment. If you still believe in this notion and ideology, you probably should seek mental health treatment and more than likely belong in a mental institution because your bullshit nonsense that men receive better treatment than you is complete fiction. It's okay to be wrong and admit your mistakes but still, if you cant accept these facts, then please don't breed and stay the fuck away from men who desire to make their names in history or at least stabilize themselves financially! Additionally, I encourage all of you feminists to get mental health treatment to cure your delusions and stop pretending to be victims!

-The author's final statement-

Female Privileges in America!
Exposing Feminist Hypocrisy!

This book was dedicated to change people's lives positively; as it has mine; because this book's intention was only to speak the truth; and nothing but the truth; discarding personal opinions and feelings. With that being said, I would like to extend a greatest **"Fuck you"** to all feminists in the United States of America, including the author's biological mother and sister for being hypcoritical feminists who were always lazy welfare recepients in their lives; and yet expected special treatment based on their gender! Again, **Fuck you!** Like all hypocritical feminists who are attempting to destroy America, you fall in that category by believing that somehow, someway, you're princesses and queens and should receive special treatment from the world for your actions. This planet would sustain itself a lot better, if all feminists, were not alive and that includes the author's biological mother and sister; because the author will never support hypocrisy, special treatment, and/or superior status for women only!

-About the author-

Female Privileges in America!
Exposing Feminist Hypocrisy!

The author is a hard-ass republican who is not afraid to get his hands dirty; and has established a reputation for writing and publishing books and/or screenplays. The author cannot stand Democrats and/or liberals/socialists for their cowardice. The author will always stand for and support the Constitution of the United States, defending this sacred document by any means necessary. The author also plays drums, composes, on his free time, washes dishes for a living at restaurants (since white liberals won't do it) and also hates baby boomers for destroying America's economy and doing nothing to help restore it while simultaenously giving women superior rights while refusing those same equal rights to men; while enjoying those rights themselves. This entire book was written to set the record straight. This book was not written for profit, but rather for publicity (in which certain biased medias will either intentionally accept or ignore this book based upon what my status is, and who that journalist or reporter is who will question my book's arguments and beliefs). The whole purpose of this book to be written was to change the laws in this country against selfish and vindictive women. One day, it will happen, until then, men, DO NOT MARRY!

P.S. FUCK FEMINISTS, DEMOCRATS , SOCIALISTS, & BABY BOOMERS & MY MOM & MY SISTER!!!

Female Privileges in America!
Exposing Feminist Hypocrisy!

Female Privileges in America!
Exposing Feminist Hypocrisy!

-Notes-

Female Privileges in America!
Exposing Feminist Hypocrisy!

Female Privileges in America!
Exposing Feminist Hypocrisy!

Female Privileges in America!
Exposing Feminist Hypocrisy!

Female Privileges in America!
Exposing Feminist Hypocrisy!

Female Privileges in America!
Exposing Feminist Hypocrisy!

Female Privileges in America!
Exposing Feminist Hypocrisy!

Female Privileges in America!
Exposing Feminist Hypocrisy!

Female Privileges in America!
Exposing Feminist Hypocrisy!

Female Privileges in America!
Exposing Feminist Hypocrisy!

Female Privileges in America!
Exposing Feminist Hypocrisy!

Female Privileges in America!
Exposing Feminist Hypocrisy!

Female Privileges in America!
Exposing Feminist Hypocrisy!

www.ingramcontent.com/pod-product-compliance
Lightning Source LLC
Chambersburg PA
CBHW020656220526
45464CB00001B/453